# Federal Presence in Nigeria
## The 'Sung' and 'Unsung' Basis for Ethnic Grievance

Festus O. Egwaikhide

Victor A. Isumonah

Olumide S. Ayodele

**CODESRIA**

Council for the Development of Social Science Research in Africa

© CODESRIA 2009

Council for the Development of Social Science Research in Africa
Avenue Cheikh Anta Diop, Angle Canal IV
P.O. Box 3304 Dakar, 18524, Senegal
Website: www.codesria.org

ISBN: 978-2-86978-259-4

Typesetter: Sériane Camara Ajavon

Cover Designer: Ibrahima Fofana

Printed by Graphiplus, Dakar, Senegal

Distributed in Africa by CODESRIA

Distributed elsewhere by African Books Collective, Oxford, UK.

Website: www.africanbookscollective.com


The Council for the Development of Social Science Research in Africa (CODESRIA) is an independent organisation whose principal objectives are to facilitate research, promote research-based publishing and create multiple forums geared towards the exchange of views and information among African researchers. All these are aimed at reducing the fragmentation of research in the continent through the creation of thematic research networks that cut across linguistic and regional boundaries.

CODESRIA publishes a quarterly journal, *Africa Development*, the longest standing Africa-based social science journal; *Afrika Zamani*, a journal of history; the *African Sociological Review*; the *African Journal of International Affairs*; *Africa Review of Books* and the *Journal of Higher Education in Africa*. The Council also co-publishes the *Africa Media Review*; *Identity, Culture and Politics: An Afro-Asian Dialogue*; *The African Anthropologist* and the *Afro-Arab Selections for Social Sciences*. The results of its research and other activities are also disseminated through its Working Paper Series, Green Book Series, Monograph Series, Book Series, Policy Briefs and the CODESRIA Bulletin. Select CODESRIA publications are also accessible online at www.codesria.org.

CODESRIA would like to express its gratitude to the Swedish International Development Cooperation Agency (SIDA/SAREC), the International Development Research Centre (IDRC), the Ford Foundation, the MacArthur Foundation, the Carnegie Corporation, the Norwegian Agency for Development Cooperation (NORAD), the Danish Agency for International Development (DANIDA), the French Ministry of Cooperation, the United Nations Development Programme (UNDP), the Netherlands Ministry of Foreign Affairs, the Rockefeller Foundation, FINIDA, the Canadian International Development Agency (CIDA), IIEP/ADEA, OECD, IFS, OXFAM America, UN/UNICEF, the African Capacity Building Foundation (ACBF), and the Government of Senegal for supporting its research, training and publication programmes.

# Contents

# List of Tables

# List of Figures

# Notes on Authors

**Festus Oisawereme Egwaikhide** is a Professor of Economics at the University of Ibadan, Nigeria, where he also got his doctorate. He was previously at the Nigerian Institute of Social and Economic Research (NISER), Ibadan, where he rose to the position of Senior Research Fellow. His teaching and research interests straddle Macroeconomics, International Economics, Public Finance and Fiscal Federalism. Egwaikhide's articles have appeared in scholarly journals in these fields of economics.

**Victor Adefemi Isumonah** is a Senior Lecturer in the Department of Political Science, University of Ibadan, Nigeria. He was the 2005/2006 Bank of Ireland Nelson Mandela Fellow at the Irish Centre for Human Rights, National University of Ireland, Galway, Republic of Ireland. He was also a Senior Research Fellow and Acting Director of Research, Centre for Advanced Social Science (CASS) Port Harcourt, Nigeria (2004-2005). His main research interests are Federalism, Political Economy, Democracy, Governance, Civil Society, Ethnicity and Minority Rights. His articles on these subjects have appeared in scholarly journals.

**Olumide S. Ayodele** is a Macroeconomist at the Policy Analysis and Research Project of the Nigerian National Assembly, Abuja. With a doctorate in Economics from the University of Ibadan, Nigeria, and over 20 years experience in the academia, he has published in many reputable journals. He has also participated in several local and international conferences, workshops, seminars and research funded by international organisations such as the AERC, CODESRIA and the EU.

# 1

# Introduction

The appropriate formula for sharing federally-collected revenue accruing mainly from the exploitation of oil in the Niger Delta area remains a challenge for the Nigerian state. This is evinced by the centrality of the revenue allocation formula in federal-state/local government fiscal relations and the widely acknowledged unfair treatment of the people from the oil-producing areas (see, for example, *The Political Bureau Report* 1987). The agitation of the Niger Delta people and others has stemmed mainly from the apparent lopsidedness of the revenue allocation formula in its vertical (sharing between federal government and states/local governments) and horizontal (sharing among the states/local governments) forms. Indeed, the protagonists, mostly from the Niger Delta area and Middle Belt of the 1990 attempted *coup d'état* against the government of General Ibrahim Babangida, alleged that resources from the south were being siphoned off to benefit the north. This lopsidedness and power sharing are at the core of the continuing federal restructuring debate.

Resistance to restructuring, mainly by elements from the north, particularly before Chief Olusegun Obasanjo, a southerner, assumed office as president of Nigeria in 1999, derived from the perceived concentration of economic power in the south. For these champions of northern interests, the proper measures of the greatest economic benefit of the Nigerian federal system are the regional distribution of industries, the representation of each geo-political region or zone in the civil service, the armed forces including the police force, the educational sector and banks in which the federal government has majority shares, etc. Still, for them, their control of political power is an indispensable instrument for securing a fair share of federal resources if they are behind the south in educational attainment. In spite of their much longer control of political power and access to resources that this apparently conferred, northerners often denied having the greater share of economic resources using, rightly, per capita benefit as the unit of measurement of gain-loss between regions.

On the other hand, southerners point to decades of the north's monopoly of political power in independent Nigeria as conclusive evidence of its greater share of national resources, sometimes citing statistics of costs of economic projects financed by the federal government for the benefit of the north to back their claim. In the life of Nigeria immediately prior to and after the attainment of political independence, the north was favoured. The north has been 'calling the shots' on issues of deciding economic and social concerns, where projects were sited, and who got the contract to execute projects. These are seen by southerners as issues of greater importance than that of majority representation in the rank and file of federal establishments.

Thus, southern agitators are ignoring the concern of their northern counterparts regarding the disadvantage caused by their educational backwardness. The south is vying for resources and harps back to the years of political domination of Nigeria by the north to reach conclusions that the north has a greater share of the country's resources. Southerners would also argue that the north gets a disproportionate share of the federal resources which are generated from their region. One example of this disproportionate sharing of federal resources involves oil exploitation and, in recent years, value added tax (VAT). This teleological attitude of the south is understandable in the light of the tendency towards the exploitation of control of political power in ethnic competition for economic resources by ethnic groups in divided societies such as Nigeria (cf. Bates 1983).

The main issue of concern within the horizontal aspect of the revenue allocation formula to the people of the oil-producing areas is the sustained de-emphasis, between the mid-1970s and 1999, of the principle of derivation. Of serious concern to the people of the oil-producing areas too are the criteria such as equality of states/local governments, population, internally-generated revenue, need and land mass whose interpretations/application often put them at a disadvantage. This is not to suggest that they are unbothered by the distribution of the benefits of federal expenditure.

Therefore, the question raised is who stands to gain the most between regions and groups (both valid units for gain-loss calculus)? To be more direct, this question has much to do with the regional impact of federal finances in Nigeria. In other words, what is the pattern of spatial distribution of federal expenditure, a measure of 'federal presence?' The relevance of such questions derives from the large chunk of revenues retained by the centre after inter-governmental sharing. The centre retained over 70 per cent of federally-collected revenue, not to mention what it did not pay into the federation account for inter-governmental sharing during much of the period focused on in this study.

This much was reflected in its share of total national expenditure. Between 1987 and 1990, its yearly average share of total national expenditure was 70 per cent (Osayinwese & Iyare 1991). There is no doubt, then, that federal expenditure is important as a channel of either equity or inequity to the various regions or states. This is because the federal government has no separate territory. The recipients of the benefits of its expenditures are regions/groups that are bearers of territorial claims and identities in competition for resources.

It is well documented, even to the point of being 'flogged', that the centre monopolizes a large chunk of expendable resources; however, the spatial distribution of federal expenditures as the other side of revenue sharing among regions has not been investigated in studies into Nigerian fiscal federalism. This is in spite of the awareness that public finance students have of the effect that federal expenditure can have on the level of economic activities on the various states. An empirical investigation is necessary to determine whether the distribution of such expenditure, a measure of federal presence, is equitable; existing literature leaves this to hypothetical speculation because of the difficulty in collecting the required data. A study of federal presence requires a comprehensive evaluation of the fiscal incidence of the federal government across space.

Nevertheless, the dearth in scientific knowledge fuels the thinking, given the ethnic character of competition for resources in Nigeria, that whichever group controls political power at the centre will benefit most from the resources held by the federal government. Feelings of being short-changed run deep among all stakeholders in the Nigerian state, despite numerous attempts at re-constructing the revenue allocation formula, and are at the root of the disillusionment with the federal system of government which for the vast majority of Nigerians has failed in practice.

## Study Aim

The literature on fiscal federalism in Nigeria is rich in the revenue allocation formula for sharing federally-collected revenue between the three tiers – federal, state, and local – of government. Much of it is devoted to the numerous reviews by fiscal commissions at the behest of successive administrations from the colonial era. Within these discussions, the principles and their weights for inter-regional (horizontal) revenue allocation have been the focus. Bienen (1983:144) summarizes this dominant orientation of the literature when he writes,

> Most discussions of political competition in Nigeria have focused on ethnic or communal conflict. Examinations of equity issues for the most part have been in terms of formulas for interregional or interstate allocations of federal funds, and the sitting of industries and infrastructure. Territory and community rather than class and occupation seem to have been the organizing concepts used in the analyses of political competition and economic distributions in Nigeria.

This is not to deny that inter-tier (vertical) revenue allocation has attracted comments; this is because since the early 1980s, it has been a major area of intergovernmental fiscal tension. Also, crude oil with both its large rental earnings and its dominance of public finance has brought the political economics of revenue allocation to the fore in academic articles.

The concern for equity implied in the principles (equality of states, population, land mass and terrain, need, and revenue generation capacity) and their weights for inter-regional (horizontal) revenue allocation regards the states and local governments' expenditures as channels for the per capita distribution of benefits, which have subsequently attracted academic research; however, the equitableness of federal government expenditure has been neglected by studies into resource allocation in Nigeria. Has the centralization of authority and resources shifted 'the focus of the debates on distribution away from inter-regional and inter-state conflict to some extent' as Bienen (1983:144)) suggests? Perhaps, given the fact that the jumble of regional competition, informed by the belief by both the dominant and minority groups that they are being shortchanged, has not received detailed investigation.

As far back as 1977, the Aboyade Technical Committee on revenue allocation noted that *federal presence* might be more important in the impact it can make on the regional distribution of physical development and concomitant per capita benefit (Federal Republic of Nigeria 1977). All the same, no study has made even a small-scale attempt to investigate the regional distribution of federal presence and its political and policy implications. The 1999 conference of the Nigeria Economic Society on fiscal federalism in Nigeria scarcely devoted an article to the important aspect of the distributional pattern of federal presence. The 2000 Onimode Ford supported study on fiscal federalism in Nigeria is also deficient in federal presence. This study aims, then, to bring more insight into the distribution of resources between the regions in Nigeria by giving attention to the distribution of federal expenditure.

### Scope of Study

The study covers the entire country, namely, the thirty-six states and the Federal Capital Territory, Abuja, which to some extent has been treated as a state. This total coverage will enhance more accurate generalizations on the pattern of resource distribution in Nigeria.

### Methods of Data Collection and Analysis

Intensive archival searches for this study involved both the collection of statistical information on federal presence in the different states of the federation and Abuja and also the pattern of geographic and demographic distribution of the beneficiaries. Federal presence is measured by the regional distribution of federal government expenditure in specific areas for which data are available. Federal presence is, of course, multifaceted. However not all facets of federal expenditure are covered by this study as a result of limited resources and lack of data.

Thus, the data collected are in respect of the location and distribution of beneficiaries of the federal civil service and parastatals, educational facilities such as universities, polytechnics, colleges of education, unity secondary schools and supervisory agencies; roads and health facilities, including teaching hospitals. Components of social overhead capital are used to the exclusion of the second part of federal expenditure, namely, directly productive activities, which form the basis of government intervention in any economy for data availability and not because the latter do not have direct economic implications for the people of the area in which they are situated. The other problem with directly productive activities of the federal government is that of differentiating between beneficiaries as to geo-ethnic regions.

The analysis is undertaken on a zonal/regional rather than state basis because of the variation in the existence of some states over time. Interestingly, regions or zones are constant boundaries.

## References

Adebayo, A. G., 1990, 'The Ibadan School and the Handling of Federal Finance in Nigeria', *Journal of Modern African Studies,* Vol. 28, No.2, pp.245-264.

Adedeji, A., 1969, *Nigeria Federal Finance,* London: Hunchinson Educational.

Ake, C. ed., 1986, *Political Economy of Nigeria,* London: Longman.

Ake, C. ed., 1994, 'Rethinking Civil Society: Toward Democratic Consolidation,' Journal of Democracy, Vol.5, No. 2, pp 4-17.

Bates, R. H., 1974, 'Ethnic Competition and Modernization in Contemporary Africa', *Comparative Political Studies,* Vol. 6, No.4, pp. 457-484.

Egwaikhide, F. O., 1996, 'The Distributional Pattern of Revenues from the Federation Account and the Principle of Derivation in Nigeria', *Administrative Change,* Vol. XXIII, Nos1-2, pp.106-115.

Federal Government of Nigeria, 1977, *Reports of the Presidential Commission on Revenue Allocation,* Vol.1: Main Report. Lagos: Federal Government Press.

Federal Government of Nigeria, 1987, *Political Bureau Report,* Lagos: Federal Government Press.

Hoetink, H., 1975, 'Resource Competition, Monopoly, and Socio-racial Diversity', in Leo A. Despres ed. *Ethnicity and Resource Competition in Plural Societies,* New York: Mounton Publishers, pp.9-25.

Ikporukpo, C. O., 1996, 'Federalism, Political Power, and the Economic Power Game: Conflict over Access to Petroleum Resources in Nigeria', in *Environment and Planning C: Government and Policy,* Vol. 14, pp.159-177.

Isumonah, V. A. (Forthcoming), 'The Fallacy of States' Dependence on the Centre'.

Mbanefoh, G. F., 1986, 'Military Presence and the Future of Nigerian Fiscal Federalism', Faculty of the Social Sciences Lecture Series, No.1 (University of Ibadan).

Musgrave, R. A., 1969, 'Theories of Federalism', *Public Finance,* Vol. 24, pp. 521-532.

Musgrave, R. A. and Musgrave, P. B., 1980, *Public Finance in Theory and Practice,* Tokyo: McGraw-Hill.

Okigbo, P. C. N., 1965, *Nigerian Public Finance,* London: Longman.

Onimode, B., 2000, 'Fiscal Federalism in Nigeria: Options for the 21st Century', Research Report.

Oyovbaire, S. E., 1985, *Federalism in Nigeria: A Study in the Development of the Nigerian State,* London: Macmillan Publishers.

Phillips, A. O., 1971, 'Nigeria's Federal Financial Experience', *Journal of Modern African Studies*, Vol. 11, No. 3, pp. 389-408.

Phillips, A. O., 1975, 'Revenue Allocation in Nigeria 1970-80', *Nigerian Journal of Economics and Social Studies*, Vol. 17, No. 1, pp. 1-28.

Rupley, L., 1981, 'Revenue Sharing in the Nigerian Federation', *Journal of Modern African Studies*, Vol. 19, No. 2, pp. 258-277.

Teriba, O., 1966, 'Nigeria Revenue Allocation Experience', *Nigerian Journal of Economics and Social Studies*, Vol. 8, No. 3, pp. 361-382.

# 2

# Ethno-Regional Competition for Resources in Nigeria

## Literature Review

As pointed out in the introductory chapter, existing literature on Nigerian fiscal federalism is engrossed by the analysis of the origins and nature of the various revenue allocation formulas, and the implications for resource distribution in Nigeria with regard to the corresponding neglect of federal expenditure and its implications for resource distribution in Nigeria. In other words, the analyses of extant works are premised on theoretical outlays, which present one-half of the totality of the mode of resource allocation in Nigeria. They thus present a partial view of the implications of national resource allocation for the different stakeholders-individuals, groups and regions especially in the light of the discriminatory practices against non-indigenes by local and state governments in the dispensation of social benefits. Thus, so far, the approach to the study of fiscal federalism in Nigeria has lacked depth and been far from rigorous.

One of the earliest of these works, Teriba (1966), reviewed the impact of the interplay or regional politics and fiscal commissions on fiscal restructurings up to 1966. Okigbo (1965) and Adedeji (1969) traced the development of Nigeria's federal fiscal structure, describing its features, and analyzed the issues of contention to extrapolate future directions. Their overriding thrust, as in Teriba's work, is the construction of a basis for revenue allocation that would meet 'national' political aspirations. This preoccupation runs through subsequent works on Nigerian fiscal federalism. Thus, Phillips (1971, 1975) examined the theoretical bases of a federal fiscal system – fiscal independence, national interest or national stability, efficiency and adequacy of resources to each level of government- and 'pitched his tents' with national interest/national stability for deciding revenue allocation formula. These works, which Adebayo (1990) referred to as the 'Ibadan School' of Nigerian federal finance for their generic and location characteristics, offer a multi-causal explanation of fiscal federalism and an economic interpretation of the much taunted states/local governments' dependence on the centre. The economic interpretation of those works and others after them, it should be noted, is not done particularly within the domain of the economics of politics. In other words, their analysis does little more than rationalize political interests and has little concern with economic rationality. Rupley (1981) has rejected the economic exposition whatever its contents and pointed out the unambiguous role played by political forces in the determination of the federal fiscal structure.

Mbanefoh (1986) analyzed the role of the military dictatorship and cataclysmic events such as the Nigerian civil war in fostering the centralization of financial resources. As Oyovbaire (1985) also noted, the federal government used decrees and acts of Parliament between 1969 and 1975 to appropriate for itself the major tax powers of the country. These authors left out the regional distribution of the centralized resources and its political and social implications for regions and groups. The current rampant violent agitations for redress by the youth of the Niger Delta area may well be the fallout of this. In response to this, Ikporukpo (1996) examined the debates on the appropriate formula for sharing oil revenue in the light of the experiences of other federations and suggested an arrangement where the federal government collects 'petroleum profit tax, while the local and state units get the revenue from the land', which, he continued, 'may be a more ideal balance of the two levels of interest that are present in a federal country' (p. 175). Ikporupko's study still left out the issues of past distributional patterns of the benefits of the federal share of revenue, not to mention their social and political implications.

The one-sided focus of these works seriously limits their explanatory power. For example, they cannot fully explain why some groups are resistant to the effort aimed at reversing the present centralist fiscal order beyond the human tendency to defend privileges or why the northern political elite was reluctant for so long to cede power to the south. Nor can they fully grasp the nature of neglect since they conceptualize it in terms of the disadvantage caused by the de-emphasis of the derivation principle, as had the agitations that have attended its perception by the people of the oil-producing areas. Reference to the powerlessness of the minorities in these areas is only a mute reference to the role the federal government could or should have played in offsetting the inadequacies of the revenue allocation formula.

The concept of *federal presence* as an important component of the resource distribution equation is conspicuously omitted! Could it be that the turmoil that has gripped the Niger Delta area is the result of an inadequate or outright lack of federal presence there? Given the disproportionate share of the federal government of the federally collected revenue, has a federal presence been equitably distributed through federal expenditure? How is equity to be defined? These are issues that are still left to speculation by the literature on Nigerian fiscal federalism. A rigorous analysis which draws on actual federal expenditure revenue is now much needed to expand the horizon of knowledge about the conflict of interests that surrounds the distribution of resources in Nigeria. Thus, the study critically examines the distribution of federal resources by means of federal expenditure, using select and representative sectors of national life.

The analysis of the spatial pattern of federal expenditures in select but broadly representative sectors for arriving at the true gain-loss calculus is undertaken in chapters 5-8. The concluding chapter synthesizes the results of the analyses for a more accurate determination of the winners and losers of the Nigerian fiscal structure and of course gives an analysis of the implications of equity or inequity in the distribution of federal presence. This is without prejudice to the issue of derivation in the sharing of federally collected revenue. Its point of departure can be found quite succinctly stated by Ukwu (1987:120):

> The way in which the Federal Government spends its own retained revenues and manipulates the various instruments of financial operation and control available to it will continue to be critical to regional development.

As Briggs (1980) also wrote, infrastructure is a huge investment that has multiple effects on its surroundings:

> Thus, federal presence is an issue. It is even more so in Nigeria because of the dominance of the ethnic conception of population in the geo-political units of Nigeria. As such, there is an ethnic and physical or resident population. Most political elites represented by state governments insist on the correspondence of their populations to the ethnic definition of their states as political/administrative units. They have shown this perception of their responsibilities being toward the ethnic population regardless of the numerical strength between it and the resident population wherever possible. Thus, both state and local governments have usually distinguished between the ethnic and resident populations of the state in areas of administration of individual benefits such as political and administrative appointments, job recruitment, scholarships and subsidies. The point being made is that if the population of geopolitical units as states were defined in terms of permanent residence and the administration of government benefits according to this view of the population, federal presence would not be such a big issue.

## Theoretical Framework

The spatial distribution of federal expenditures makes a particular difference in the regional sharing of national resources and the overall politics of resource allocation. As early scholars of fiscal sociology – Joseph Schumpeter and Rudolf Goldscheid – wrote, fiscal politics (the pattern of government spending) is the more important determinant of state form and resultant inter-group relations than capitalism and modern rational bureaucracy as Marx and Weber separately claimed for the emergence of modern Western Europe (Moore 2004).

Regional competition for resources may arise from the differences in resource endowments between a federation's constituent parts. It follows that if those who control political power at the centre are from the poor regions, the sharing of national revenue will tend to reduce regional fiscal disparities. In other words, revenue allocation tends to be driven by fiscal equalization rather than an efficiency motive. Allocation is carried out to satisfy the economic interests of the dominant group controlling political power (Hoetink 1975). This is a major source of conflict and instability in many African states. The control of political power with the aim of using it to appropriate economic resources for the development and benefit of one's own region becomes the standard mode of regional competition. Hence, the high correlation that can be observed between the control of political power and the control of economic resources in Nigeria (Ake 1986, 1994).

As Bates (1974) has argued, the group that is disadvantaged tends to mobilize its ethnic identity to demand redistribution in its favour. Simultaneously, the group that is advantaged mobilizes its members to resist redistribution of both political and economic powers. This is noticeable from the unsettling contentions over the offshore and onshore dichotomy Bill/Act between the minorities in the oil-producing areas and the rest of Nigeria.

In the setting of regional competition, the regional group may be based on ethnic identity or on what Otite (1990) terms neo-ethnicity and para-ethnicity. In his words, neo-ethnicity 'thrives on the notion of wider common identity and common fate and visions of shared politico-cultural ideology, with a dynamic content characterized by interactions involving religion, contiguous ethnic territory, statism and sustained tradition of old political cleavages and alliances' (p.127). On the other hand, para-ethnicity is 'anchored on statism and territoriality while component groups still particularize their exclusive relationships' (p.129). He gives examples of these types of ethnic formations as the regional Committees of Elders proliferating in Nigeria.

Is it valid to speak of ethno-regional competition for resources with so much evidence of individual accumulation, say, in Nigeria? Bienen (1981:135) suggests that one way to knowing the elite's thinking about the structure of inequality is to 'look directly at the attitudes of civil servants and military personnel toward the distribution of income' through 'interviews and by analysis of statements of self-definition of roles and interests.'

### Individual Private Accumulation and Ethno-Regional Competition

Ethno-regional competition may escape notice if at the outset the objective is to demonstrate the individual material advantage underlying the group consciousness, as is Takaya's focus in the 'Kaduna Mafia'. Takaya (1987) asserts that the Kaduna Mafia developed as an individual political survival strategy. This included the mobilization around one united north involving selective rewards, government policy in favour of its inner core, and the attempted conversion of political power into economic power through private enterprises that from the beginning will thrive on 'bleeding' the public, etc. Takaya's description of the aim of the

Kaduna Mafia unambiguously portrays individual interest as the sole motive of the group consciousness that it embodies.

Besides, regional competition for resources could be denied simply because of the prevalence of individual interethnic competition conducted either straightforwardly or under the cover of ethnic groups and associations. Thus, with huge evidence of regional competition advanced in his work, Nnoli (1980) denies it as a distinct mode of competition and suggests that it is a mask for private accumulation or class privilege (cf. Sklar 1967). He argues: 'By presenting politics as an interethnic struggle for socio-economic resources, these classes camouflage intra-class struggle for the division of the national wealth that is inimical to the interest of the underprivileged classes, the working class, and the poor farmers who constitute the vast majority of the population' (Nnoli 1980:177).

Similarly, Joseph (1981) emphasizes the individual form of appropriation while acknowledging a group (communal) type of graft as distinct from an egoistic (individual) graft, to demonstrate the workings of a pyramidal structure that patron-client networks have. Thus, he describes Nigerian politics of the Second Republic, 1979-1983, as 'ethno-clientelism', the use of office in a 'dyadic (two-person) relationship' for the distribution of resources in exchange for support. In other words, there is strictly no group (regional) pattern of struggle for resources, which, in consequence, generates ethnic grievances and mobilization. The beneficiary in his prebendal perspective is predominantly the individual. Hence for him, the appropriation of public resources justified as a share of the national pie is for personal use, not for the benefit of an ethno-regional group. That is why he virtually dismissed the distinction Ekeh (1975) makes between primordial and civic public in his effort at putting meaning into his theory of two publics in Africa, which makes reference to group competition for resources. Yet, group competition for resources is separable from the individual appropriation of public resources for personal use. This has empirical support as will be demonstrated in the study carried out by Joseph for both the individual and group (or communal) dimensions of competition (see details in Isumonah and Egwaikhide 2005).

In Nigeria, pillaging of public resources by individuals has occurred through petroleum smuggling and bunkering of crude oil and commercial fraud or what Lewis (1996) describes as the manipulation of government economic policies to facilitate massive diversion of public resources for individual enrichment. For example, as much as $12.2 billion was misappropriated between 1988 and 1993 perhaps through 'dedicated accounts earmarked for special projects' according to an official report (Lewis 1996:91). Such appropriations of public resources for personal use cannot render a non-issue, regional competition for resources. In any case, some of the diversions of public funds reflect discernible ethnic patterns (Lewis 1996). Where disaggregating corrupt benefits regionally is a problem, it can be estimated from the distribution, over time, of key policy makers by region and well-known names of individual beneficiaries of corruption through inflated contracts. Why? Turner (1978) explains that in Nigeria's commercial capitalism, profits are made more through 'market control' and kickbacks in institutional trading transactions in which government agents decide which firm is given an offer.

The presence of opposing political forces could also be the basis for dismissing the reality of regional competition for resources. If rivalries within a dominant group cannot be used to deny its dominion over a polity, a multiplicity of orientations and motif forces of political behaviour does not suggest that it cannot be explained in terms of an overriding factor such as regional/group competition. Consequently, regional competition for resources does not presuppose that the group is monolith in orientation. Dissenting elements within the group counted as a unit in competition may exist. Aminu Kano's Northern Elements Progressive Union (NEPU) and Middle Belt Congress (MBC) were such 'elements of opposition behind the façade of political unity' of the north under the Northern Peoples Congress (NPC) (Schwarz 1968:129). A region is counted as a unit in spite of the presence of such opposition elements on the basis of the orientation of the dominant political group or the balance of the contending forces within the region. As the dominant political force of the north from the decolonizing years to independence years up until 1966, the orientation of NPC is what matters in characterizing the north's politics of that period. This showed regional competition for resources. For example, the 1962-68 National Development Plan indicated quite clearly NPC's determination to exploit its control of the centre to benefit its Northern Region (Akinyele 2004).

A variety of orientations within the segment of a polity adjudged in competition with others as one unit reminds us of the fact that an overriding motif force does not have a straight path in a society with complex individual and group character and interest. Interests converge and diverge now and then, reflecting the dynamism of the political arena. Even in that setting, it is possible to identify the central pursuit of a group as the directing theme of the motivation.

Therefore, where numerous variants of interethnic competition (individual and group) exist, what is important to conclude on the side of group competition is whether it is the dominant theme as in a drama that naturally has many scenes and even sub-themes but one main theme. A group's interest is hardly self-evident and, therefore, cannot be expressed straightforwardly because it is a permutation of conflicting individual interests including: personal ego, which leads the person to reach out in alliance formation to other groups by which he/she may be seen to be carving a trans-ethnic image for himself/herself; need for personal gratification from one of another ethnic group; and undisguised ethnic group objective. All of this should be seen as different scenes or sub-themes, some of which serve the purpose of adding sophistication to the drama or story they describe. As the dominant theme, regional competition for resources is the central political purpose pursued in a variety of self-seeking ways.

*The Logic of Regional Competition for Resources*

Everywhere, in both developed and underdeveloped societies, Premdas (1995:1) notes that 'ethnic maps' in the heads of citizens serve among others 'to evaluate projects and programmes and actions of governments in general.' This does not imply ethno-regional competition for resources in all societies. Indeed, there is no evidence of ethno-regional competition for resources everywhere. More explicitly, that is to say that group inequality 'tends to command greater attention than the problem of inequality among income classes or generalized households' (Aboyade 1983:323). It is further to highlight the salience of space in the distribution problem as is well acknowledged by social scientists. For example, American economist Richard Musgrave (1969) writes that social goods have spatial characteristics. Similarly, the first generation Nigerian economist, Ojetunji Aboyade (1983:318) notes, 'the development process does not operate in a spatial vacuum. Production, distribution and exchange among various units of an economic system take place in space'. Ted R. Gurr (1993), an American political scientist inverts the distribution problem with the assertion that inequalities have group/regional dimensions. But how does inequality in geographical space count toward ethno-regional competition for resources?

To begin with, group inequalities do not have the same causes in all states. Where they are in two states, they do not necessarily lead to the same political responses. Hence, to understand or explain divergent political responses of two polities to particular inequalities, it is important to consider the perception of these inequalities by the polities. Therefore, the politicization of such inequalities, which turns into a unique mode of competition, can be located not only in their processes of emergence but also in their perception in a given polity.

Regional inequalities may result, according to Darendorf, from differential achievements of social norms (cited in Moynihan 1979). This refers to the differences in group values in relation to certain social goods. Even when inequality is self-inflicted from less value being attached to a social good, the group may seek rectification outside of itself as may be said of the northern part of Nigeria in relation to the south, in respect of education, with a definite consequence for resource allocation. In Nigeria, the differences between north and south in respect of the value attached to education can be seen from the disparities in school enrolments. This means that 'the North has only 0.01 per cent of 0.4 per cent of Nigeria's population enrolled in higher education' even though past population counts showed its greater population size.[1]

When inequality in educational attainment was perceived, there were two possible responses. One was the positive effort to achieve parity. Such is the case of the Igbo who through self-help projects and programmes, including fund raising for the education of promising family members and the building of schools, as shown in Table 1, achieved parity in educational development with the Yoruba in the 1960s (Abernethy 1969). The other is the demand for use of ascriptive criteria for resource allocation as the northern leaders did during the 1950s when the eventuality of independence of Nigeria and the unequal educational attainments between north and south dawned on them. The response of the north contributed greatly to the adoption of a quota system and later to the federal character principle for dispensing the national government's benefits to individuals and resources on the basis of ethno-regional groupings represented initially by regions and later states.

**Table 2.1: Students in Training at Intermediate and Higher Levels by Provinces of Origin, 1966**

| Province | Intermediate Level | Higher Level (University) |
|---|---|---|
| Eastern | 558 | 2,031 |
| Western | 550 | 1,728 |
| Mid-Western | 92 | 380 |
| Northern | 176 | 369 |
| Federal | 12 | 24 |
| Total | 1,388 | 4,532 |

Source: National Register of Students 1988 – Potential High Level Manpower (Senior and Intermediate Categories) showing Distribution by Name, Place of Study, Field of Study, Provinces, and Sponsoring Agent, Federal Ministry of Education, Lagos.

These distributive criteria turned weakness into an advantage that was to be defended in perpetuity; and strength into a weakness to be protected in retaliation. Thus, the groups that could not compete on merit have found it more worthwhile to cling to the original definition of the ethno-regional group. In retaliation, those groups that could compete on merit have also engaged in discriminatory practices against elements of other states categorized as non-indigenes. These differently motivated defensive practices solidify the region as recipient of benefits, and therefore, regional competition for resources held by the centre.

### The Evolution of Ascriptive Principles

A subtle distinction can be made between democratically crafted and imposed ascriptive principles of distribution in terms of the effect on the development of modes of struggle for resources. An ascriptive criterion is democratic if it is reached by consensus. If inequality arises from the application of a democratically decided ascriptive criterion, it is not likely to generate intense acrimony. This is because it holds the prospect of reducing the perception of an emergent inequality as inflicted by the 'other'. Sufferers of such inequalities are likely to search for causes elsewhere including whether they are self-inflicted and as a result, to re-channel their energies away from avid ethno-regional perception. An imposed ascriptive institutional arrangement for distribution instantly intensifies divisions and struggles between both advantaged and disadvantaged groups.

Yet, flouting democratically decided ascriptive institutional arrangements makes them inadequate *ab initio* and deepens ethno-regional divisions and competition.

In such circumstances, the groups have no confidence in constitutional guarantees for the proportional distribution of offices and projects such as the 'federal character principle' contained in Section 14(3) of the *1999 Constitution of the Federal Republic of Nigeria* and remain anxious over the ethnic composition of the executive structures of government that implement them.

Groups with less capacity to compete on merit naturally favour and advocate ascriptive criteria for distribution. Having successfully mobilized 'northern solidarity,' the Hausa-Fulani proceeded to demand and entrench a quota system as the basis of recruitment into federal structures when it became clear that if the British, as they were planning, allocated resources on universal principles, the Hausa-Fulani would lose out (Young 1976).

However if historically emphasis is placed on production, implying that the forces of production determine relations between individuals, merit eventually takes root as the dominant distributive criterion. In that case, inequalities between groups are not perceived absolutely as the results of the exploitation of the disadvantaged group(s) by the advantaged ones(s). Thus, the organizational form of society in terms of production is influential in the development or shaping of distributive criteria, the character of the competition between groups and the problems of nation-building.

This organizational form of society is what is confused by some scholars and politicians with the evolution or the way and manner the Nigerian state was created. For example, Adedeji (1969) writes: 'Had the two parts of Nigeria been federated rather than amalgamated, the assignment of duties and responsibilities would have been more rationally accomplished, and the allocation of revenue and tax powers more equitably distributed' (p.33). This is akin to the regrets over amalgamation carried by such descriptions of Nigeria as the 'mistake of 1914' and 'Nigeria is a mere geographical expression', which are an unwitting permissive justification for the failure of Nigeria to achieve integration and development.

If Nigeria has failed in integration or in kick-starting development, the cause cannot simply be how it came into existence since several other states, some of which have achieved greater integration and significant development, were born in the same way. The problem is rather to be found in its unyielding organizational form to the needs of development and integration. Nowhere has the federal charter been concluded in a single negotiation. There is evidence in Nigeria's political history to show an awareness of the inconclusive nature of the initial federal charter. After amalgamation, the regions asserted their essence as components of the federation in their demand for the federal fiscal arrangement and got it in varying degrees at different historical junctures. Hence, Nigeria moved, as Adedeji (1969) himself reports, from limited centralization of the 1914-1926 period through limited decentralization under the Richards Constitution of 1946, to decentralization between 1954 and 1959 when the 1954 Constitution gave more tax powers to the regions. The military intervention in Nigerian politics and the civil war that ensued set in motion expenditure displacement and the concentration of resources at the centre (Mbanaefoh 1986). Specifically, the military concentrated resources in the centre by reducing the weight attached to derivation in the sharing of revenue collected by the centre and increasing the centre's share of tax profits (Tobi 1989). Thus, Nigeria's political space has not always been frozen as borne out by the constitutional reforms that produced the substantially accepted 1954 Constitution. What has happened is that the dominant groups have frozen the political space to disallow constituent units of the federation to remake it to suit their current needs.

Whatever the degree of potency of constitutional provisions in practice, they remain first reference points, even more so when what they are, rather than their legitimacy, is not in dispute. In a federal state, the relationship between the centre and constituent units of the federation derives from legal and constitutional instruments, and 'the dynamics of political, economic, and social processes' (Oyovbaire 1985:2). Its elements, which help to classify the federation as centralized or decentralized are the 'right to action' including the right to exploit and distribute resources and the 'recognized sanctions or instruments of coercion' (Oyovbaire 1985:6). However in reality, it is the force of the right to spend that is the key issue rather than the right to collect revenue in the relationship between the centre and constituent units of a federation. The level of government that collects particular revenues does not matter except where transparency is suspect.

Take a few examples. In 1975, the United States' federal share of total collected revenue was 58.2 per cent while the state and municipal shares were respectively 23.8 per cent and 17.7 per cent. However after sharing through transfers, municipal, state and federal revenue shares were 48.4 per cent, 21.1 per cent and 30.4 per cent respectively. In other words, the municipal governments took the lion share of total revenue. Besides, the federal share of expenditure, in line with tradition, went mostly into the 'reduction of regional and interpersonal inequalities' (Ukwu 1987:115). The revenue and expenditure distribution among the three levels of the Canadian government is similar. Federal, provincial and municipal revenue shares in 1967 were 52 per cent, 32 per cent and 16 per cent respectively. However, expenditure shares were 35 per cent, 24 per cent and 41 per cent for municipal, provincial and federal governments respectively (cited in Ukwu 1987). The centre's share of total taxes has fallen in India and Brazil. Indeed, 'the 1998 Brazilian Constitution accelerated the decline in centrally retained tax revenue' (Tanzi 1996:307). 'In Australia, the tax bases of the federal and lower level governments (state and local governments) are divided in such a way that the federal government receives about two thirds of the total government revenues. In terms of expenditure, however, the federal government spends only one third of the total government revenues' (Ma 1997:9). As demonstrated in Chapter 3, Nigeria's federal government has been taking the lion share of both collected revenue and expenditure, making federal presence an issue of more serious concern to regional groups than in other federations.

### Citizenship Rights' Practices

Constitutional rules on citizenship rights and administrative practices give further insight into how ethno-regional competition for resources assumes a dominant tendency. In this regard, the United States of America and Nigeria provide an illuminating contrast. Article IV, Section 2, of the U.S. Constitution provides that 'The Citizens of each State shall be entitled to all Privileges and Immunities of Citizens in the several States'. This is accurately reflected in political practice. As Nathan and Hoffman (1991:34) testify: 'U.S. citizens move freely from one state to another, can buy property, settle, and seek work in a location of their own choosing. The modern welfare state makes public provisions (Social Security in the U.S.) and disability benefits fully portable... Many laws and regulations pertaining to working conditions, minimum wages, and labor organization are uniform among the states'. Hence, in the U.S., competition for resources is more diffused, drawing together interest groups, 'political action committees' in Congress, mayors, governors and other state officials forming intergovernmental lobbies in unstable coalitions (Conlan 1998).

In Section 15(3) of the 1999 Constitution of Nigeria it is stated that, for the purpose of promoting national integration, it shall be the duty of the State to:

(a) provide adequate facilities for and encourage free mobility of people, goods and services throughout the Federation;

(b) secure full residence rights for every citizen in all parts of the Federation.

However in Section 318(1), an indigene 'in a State' is described as 'a person either of whose parents or any of whose grand parents was a member of a community indigenous to that State.' Perhaps on the basis of this, states and local governments have continued to practice discriminatory policies against those identified as non-indigenes in employment and distribution of other benefits. In consequence, they have penalized those more responsive to the stated objective of the constitution in Section 15(3a), that is, movement across native authorities that a capitalist economy such as Nigeria naturally impels (Mamdani 2000). An effect of the contradictory provisions of the constitution and unbending preference for the description of an indigene by the constitution in the practices of state and local governments are their reinforcement of the cultural determination of nationality and citizenship (Isumonah 2003). There is in consequence bifurcated citizenship in which a person is not viewed as a citizen where s/he resides outside the state or local government defined as his/her homeland. What follows this is the building of attachment to this homeland, though distant. This is notwithstanding the new tendency of those defined by the state and local governments as non-indigenes to stay back and 'fight it out' rather than head for 'home' in their violent encounters with the so-called indigenes (Mamdani 2000).

It is not surprising that there is emphasis on the continuation, even extension, of the distributive foundation of the Nigerian state in several other tendencies. While for instance, the United States' federalism has sought among other objectives to increase efficiency and enhance innovation through regional competition (Nathan and Hoffman 1991), on the other hand in Nigeria, the relationship between the states has been organized around the distribution of rents from the extractive sector of the economy under the control of the centre.

As Oyovbaire (1985:164/165) rightly puts it, the emphasis 'over the years has been not so much that of allocating powers and jurisdiction over taxation, as of allocating the revenue produced by certain taxes between the various governments of the federation and thereby dealing with the question of socio-economic disparities and development.' The Nigerian federation was founded on the basis of taking from one grudging part to give to another grudging part, rather than cheerful sharing between parts. Put differently, it was not founded on the complementary sharing of independently created wealth.

### The Absence of National Ideology of Development

Unlike the U.S. and India, Nigeria's federal system is short of other sources of inspiration such as ideology and 'science as the reason for the state' (Nandy 1988:3). The role of a national ideology in the orientation of nationals is evident from its definition by Graf. According to him, a national ideology:

> may be seen as the set of ideas from which the individual perceives himself, a set of ideas that lay down rules of correct behaviour and provide justification for the behaviour of the citizens. The purpose and ideals of society, the direction in which the nation is going, and the norms and values to be upheld in changing circumstances within the life of the nation would be embraced in the national ideology (Graf 1979:43).

President Olusegun Obasanjo has, on a number of occasions, told his fellow countrymen and women that Nigeria does not have nuclear aspirations nor is she intending to go to the moon. It is implicit in these reminders that the scope of rivalry for the dominant elite is not wider than in Nigeria. Were the scope different so that the elite perceived science as the reason for the state, the nature of competition would probably be different in Nigeria. Their preoccupation is with instituting and maintaining the predominance of the state 'in the major avenue of upward mobility, status, power and wealth' (Callaghy quoted in Diamond 1987:583).

This can be discerned from the tendency toward centralization and its intellectual rationalizations of both the power of allocation of resources between constituent units and that of the overall spending in the centre. Generals Muhammed and Obasanjo took the centralization of resources begun by General Gowon to new heights with numerous 'anti-federalist policies and practices' including the enforcement of a uniform model of local government administration, taxation system and sole ownership of universities (Ekeh 2000:10). Generals Babangida and Abacha went beyond them to create special agencies and accounts deliberately run to disadvantage some sections of the country (Isumonah & Egwaikhide 2005).

As centralization progressed, the goal of those demanding their states changed. It was initially for political autonomy. As such, all the dominant groups in the three regions resisted their balkanization for the purpose of granting self-rule to the minorities in their midst. After enforced balkanization in 1967, the goal shifted to the state as an instrument of development. The need to bring government closer to all Nigerians became the justification for the creation of states and local governments. This strengthened these units of government as an instrument of sharing resources, changing them into 'entry points for elites' seeking access to more public resources (Onyeoziri 2002; Jinadu 2002; Reno 1993:71). With so much weight (e.g., 40 per cent in revenue sharing) attached to equality of the units in the distribution and utilization of federal development projects, including the location of, and admission of candidates into, federal educational institutions', the struggle by groups to increase their number of states and local governments raged out of control (Suberu 1991:501). The north, that was most vehement for the fact that it did not in the least advocate the creation of states for minorities in other regions, used its control of the federal government between 1976 and 1999 to create more states and local governments disproportionately for itself as it was concentrating resources in the centre and espousing principles based essentially on those political units for their allocation.

Thus, when states' creation shifted from a geo-ethnic balancing instrument in the 12-state structure which gave north and south six states each in 1967 to one of access to federal government controlled resources, northern political leaders in the states creation exercises of 1976, 1987, 1991, and 1996 gave the north 19 to the south's 17 states. They also gave the north more local governments with 414 to the south's 355 local governments (First Schedule, Section 3 of the *1999 Constitution of the Federal Republic of Nigeria*).

The wide variation in the distribution of local governments among southern states is also reflective of the access and connection to federal power during those years of military rule. The metamorphosis of the Akoko area in the Western region into local governments graphically illustrates this. While the Akoko-Edo Division part of it remains one local government in Edo State, its sister part in Ondo State is now bifurcated into six local governments. Within Edo State, the lot of Akoko-Edo local government is also illustrative. It came into being as such with Etsako local government from Afenmai Division. While it remains one, Etsako has been split into three. Etsako's two local governments increased to three in 1998 undoubtedly by means of their kin, Rear Admiral Mike Akhigbe's number 2 position in the government of General Abdulsalam Abubakar.

In the distribution of local governments, Kano State, which contributes nothing to the federation account, has 44 local governments 'which routinely collect 44 portions of revenue shared by local councils every month' while Delta state which accounts for 35 per cent of oil and gas revenue has only 25 councils (Darah 2002:57). Thus, Kano State has one-third of 122 councils of all six South-South states, which account for over 95 per cent of oil revenue in Nigeria.

Prospects of further gain impel the groups that have benefited from previous states and local government creation exercises to demand more. Groups that gained nothing or less from the emerging distribution of new states and local governments are demanding theirs. Minorities of the Niger Delta for whom the use of other principles such as population and land mass are equally hideous have lately demanded parity with the adoption of 'water mass', 'rain' and 'flooding' as principles of revenue allocation. They have also expressed concern over the channelling of federally controlled resources to fight desertification in the north while to them, ocean encroachment, 'oceanification', which does affect them, does not even come up for mention as a problem.

Intellectual arguments have been canvassed in support of the current centralist order. A recent example is the exchange between the late Dr. Bala Usman (northerner) and Professor Peter P. Ekeh (of South-South geopolitical zone) in which Ekeh refuted Usman's argument that this order has its basis in the political and ecological history of Nigeria on the pages of Nigerian newspapers and the internet (Isumonah 2004). Long before now, Aboyade and Adedeji, both of Western Nigerian origin, argued that 'derivation had done much to poison inter-governmental relations and hamper a sense of national unity' (quoted in Adebayo 1990:254); and 'derivation is the main cause of interregional rivalry and conflict' respectively (cited in Stolper 1970:252). However, the de-emphasis on derivation has festered resentment of the disadvantaged, mostly minority groups, of the oil-producing Niger Delta.

There is in fact no point in the argument that all regions/groups will not get an equal share from emphasizing or de-emphasizing the derivation principle in reve-nue allocation. What is important to consider is the process of arriving at a given principle. It is sanguine to argue that if derivation is mutually adopted, it will not cause so much dissatisfaction to groups that receive less from the resources. This is because acceptance of derivation by such groups could have emanated from the conviction that the groups that benefit from it deserve it.

Unfortunately, the centre is averse to a national consensus as the right way to arrive at an allocation formula that will perhaps accommodate the derivation principle with a considerable weight attached to it. Its main feeder, dominant regional politics, continues to prefer the now-entrenched market-distorting federalism. A federation is market-preserving if economic forces determine intergovernmental fiscal relations. If those given to clientelist politics at the local level are over-represented in the central government, as is the case with Nigeria, the federation will tend to be market-distorting rather than market-preserving and characterized by a high level of arbitrariness in the allocation of resources (Wibbels 2003).

A summary of recommendations of constitutional and fiscal commissions or committees shows the inclination to preserve the sole distributive function of Nigeria's federal structure in spite of its well demonstrated dysfunctional effect. An example of this is the practice of taking resources from one part, thanks to the underplaying of the role of derivation, and allocating them discriminatorily against those who hail from where they are taken. This is not to deny a disposition to continue similar discriminatory practices of the state and local governments of the sources of these resources against those declared as non-indigenes. The latter can be interpreted as the effect of a chain-reaction. Bold recommendations against this contradiction have been rejected. The first was by the Committee on Citizenship of the 1977/78 Constituent Assembly that the right to the benefits of state and local governments should be based on residency rather than on the current *indigene* basis. The same recommendation by the Political Bureau (1987) has not been implemented. The demand for increased weight of the derivation principle by oil-producing states of the Niger Delta has also been rejected. In the quest for centralized resources, the functionality of these recommendations has been rapidly missed by the more powerful beneficiaries of Nigeria's distributive federalism. Having forcefully appropriated resources wherever they are found in Nigeria, the centre has taken the Nigerian federation far away from any known concept of federalism; from K.C. Wheare's equal and coordinate governments, and William Livingston's preserving identified federal qualities, to 'co-operative federalism' (Elazar 1987).

### Effects of the Politics of Production

The importance of the politics of production and distribution in the development of institutional arrangements for distribution is evident from perspectives on various aspects of the African political situation.

Nnoli (1980) notes that ethnic competition between individuals for resources along linguistic and communal lines immediately followed colonial power-instigated contact between Nigerian cultural groups entangled in uncomplimentary socio-economic relations. Modernization concomitant with new infrastructure, equally valued but unevenly distributed between cultural groups, sharpened the differences. The colonial economy, together with an international division of labour, fostered by global capitalism, aggravated the situation by assigning Africans the role of distribution of the finished goods. Hence, the *bourgeoisie* that developed was dependent on the distribution of available goods and services rather than on the production and creation of new wealth through innovativeness and creativity. In addition, the colonial economy by its harshness encouraged close ties with ethno-regional roots by migrants from the rural to colonial (urban) centres.

With ethnic-based competition between individuals already active, regional competition for resources only needed a structural framework to begin. The federal political arrangement, which by nature solidifies diversity, came to be that frame. The colonial government began to provide such a frame by preaching and inculcating diversity in the Nigerian people. It achieved this with 'a deliberate strategy of dividing the 'colonized' in order to ensure their control and ultimately to frustrate attempts to build a united nation' (cited in Gana 2003:21). It employed numerous tactics in this regard: pursued the policy of separate settlements; used Land and Native Rights Ordinance of 1910 to keep southern entrepreneurs out of the north, maintained northern and southern parts of Nigeria as separate entities until 1946 even after which it made no effort at integrating them; promoted sectional differences in the political process (e.g., electoral politics, manipulation of elections and census figures in favour of the north), and fostered the disarticulation of the economy. Indeed, the 1946 Richards Constitution regionalized politics such that when the 1954 Constitution introduced the federal political framework, exclusivist claims within each of the constituent units were the order. These are evident from the strategies of each regional party in the context of regionalized Nigeria as identified by Nnoli (1980).

First, engage in 'intensive mobilization of the ethnic homeland to ensure its monolithic support at times of elections' (Nnoli 1980:159). Second, widen the political base to include the whole region. Third, gain ethnic supremacy through winning elections and controlling the regional governmental power. Fourth, use regional governmental power to eliminate all forms of opposition. Fifth, sponsor the opposition of minorities in other regions against their governments while keeping its region's monolithic design intact. Sixth, win federal elections or go into alliance with the winning party in order to secure resources for its region. Seventh, divert resources to its region and gain influence in it while weakening the influence of other political parties in their respective regions. In sum, the strategy of each party subordinated the unity of the country to the interests of the region. Regional political and also petit and comprador bourgeois leaders threatened secession from Nigeria whenever regional interests were at risk. 'The regionalization of the public service reflected the interethnic struggle for national resources and also released a pent-up energy for furthering it' (Nnoli 1980:190).

However colonialism did not by itself foreclose a federal bargain that would place emphasis on the allocation of tax powers with an implicit message of reward for hard work and shift the concern or preoccupation of component units of Nigeria away from what they could get from revenue from certain taxes particularly oil exploitation and imported goods. It assumed a logic of its own from the interplay of political forces. Part of this was the emergence of the centre-skewed power structure that enabled it to acquire the sole power to assign the most important tax powers that remain extremely difficult to reassign by the many concerned constituent units.

In Ekeh's seminal work on the structure of the African society, he writes that tribalism (read ethnicity) 'is the direct result of the dialectical confrontation between the two publics' – primordial and civic (Ekeh 1975:109). The conflict between these sometimes overlapping publics, he explains, centres on the sharing of resources in the civic public domain. This implies that ethno-regional competition for resources is implicit in a society divided into such two publics. The form of this competition is determined by attenuating factors. One attenuating factor is whether a given civic (public) property is perceived as a resource for the enhancement of the welfare of members of a primordial public and not in terms of its core values. Federal universities, which Ekeh cites as an example of the site of ethno-regional competition, are not so simple, as he explains, because of the insecurity of ethnic elements within them, but fundamentally because of their perception as a resource for primordial groups rather than as sites for the development of knowledge or the enunciation and promotion of merit. As the primordial public brings more and more civic establishments into its perception as resources to be exploited for its separate benefit as a result of the dominance of distribution over production, ethno-regional competition for resources takes on uniqueness.

As such, no chances are taken by well-mobilized groups. In their eyes, appointments and promotions in the public service including civil service, customs, immigration, government agencies and armed forces (army, navy and air force) and the police all affect regions' share in the national wealth. Their 'ethnic sponsors' (Bienen 1983), 'ethnic watchers' (Nnoli 1980) or ethnic guardians take interest in and actively participate in those processes. When recruitment is over, these ethnic guardians monitor the career advancement of their ethnics. They influence those who matter to ensure that their ethnics are promoted on a regular basis. For example, they played a prominent role in the 2003 promotions in the armed forces (interview with an army colonel, November 3, 2003, Ibadan). These ethnic guardians have to be knowledgeable about the inventory of their 'boys' in major government establishments as the most influential traditional rulers in northern Nigeria have been since the north's most highly regarded political godfather, Ahmadu Bello, realized the need to plant northern ethnics in the army for the protection of northern interests. The high regard that traditional rulers have come to enjoy among fellow ethnics derives from this function as promoters of their people in their careers.

As many writers have pointed out, Nigeria is a clientelist, specifically, patrimonial, state (e.g., Joseph 1983, 1987; Chabal and Daloz 1999; Reno 1983). Patrimonialism expresses the lack of institutionalization of the state or the 'political instrumentalization of disorder' for the personal benefit of political elites and their 'kith and kin, clients, communities, regions or even religion' (Chabal and Daloz 1999:15). In a patrimonial society, available resources are prey to intense competition because patrimonialism inhibits the capacity of the state to generate revenue 'because the political requirements of control and reward undercut the rational prerequisites of economic activity' (Kasfir 1983:15). To complete the framework, the two necessary conditions for group competition proposed by

Hoetink (1975:10) are present, namely, 'predominance of ascriptive loyalties over economic ones and the existence of several ascriptive groups that are sufficiently equal in power to engage in a competitive relationship.' Hence, in the same vein, the predominance of pluralist principles for the organization of society that group competition for resources has engendered has turned ethnic groups in Nigeria into political groups, as Salamone (1975) suggests.

## Conclusion

Some of the criticisms that Forrest (1995) has advanced against prebendal and primordial perspectives apply equally to group competition for the resources perspective expounded here. First, they leave out economic activities geared to private accumulation outside the state arena. Second, they neglect forms of political conflicts which have nothing to do with material concerns and access to state power. As earlier noted, the perspective of group competition for resources does not claim that there are no activities geared to private accumulation nor does it deny the existence of political conflicts not connected to access to resources controlled by the state. It proposes that a pattern of struggle for resources toward group benefits can be distinguished as group competition for resources from diverse economic activities including those undertaken for private accumulation, which had sometimes been stated as being in the interest of the group within a plural state.

The use of the group's name to reap huge private accumulation has often been the basis for dismissing as self-seekers individuals observed to have fallen out of favoured positions of government patronage (a plum job or contracting for projects), when they begin to complain about their group's loss or disadvantage. The Ogoni human and environmental rights activist, Ken Saro-Wiwa was accused of this by rivals within Ogoni and by government officials (Isumonah 2004). This cannot be because such complaints can find an objective basis such that dismissing them as selfish even on a cursory view begs the question. In this regard, we argue that it is simplistic to explain individuals' complaints about their ethnic group's or region's disadvantage in the context of regional competition for resources as intra-class or grumbling over falling out of class favour. Indeed, private accumulation has been viewed by groups as an instrument for securing resources for them as groups. For example, 58 senators of northern origin made the release from detention of Mohammed Abacha who was alleged by the government not to be cooperating with it to recover his father's stolen sum of $2.6 billion 'a condition for truce' between President Obasanjo and the National Assembly, which was pressing impeachment charges against him (*Tell*, Lagos, September 16, 2002:12).

This is not to say that the struggle for resources is inflexibly regionalist because a variety of forces shape political outcomes. There have been times when other considerations have affected orientation away from what each region stands to gain or lose in the struggle. For example, the National Assembly rejected the 50 per cent contribution to the NDDC from the 13 per cent derivation revenue due to the oil-producing states in the bill seeking to set it up that President Olusegun Obasanjo originally sent to it on the grounds that accepting it was unconstitutional. Later, when it passed a substantially modified bill on the onshore-offshore dichotomy for the purposes of revenue allocation, which the President initiated as a political solution to the dire consequences of the Supreme Court judgment on resource control for some of the oil-producing states with provisions markedly favourable to these states, Obasanjo vetoed it (for details of judgment see Ayodele, Egwaikhide, Isumonah & Oyeranti 2005). Then, regionalist consideration entered into the struggle since the National Assembly failed to use its two-thirds majority constitutional power to pass the bill into law. Northern members of the National Assembly were even blamed by some northern spokespersons for not using their vote to block the passage of the Bill that had a very clear effect of reducing the north's share of 'national' revenue. However, an act abrogating the onshore-offshore dichotomy and clearly intended to benefit the oil-producing states, particularly South-South, was enacted unencumbered by concern strictly with regional interests. It may well have been passed as part of a strategic political calculation for enhancing a regional political advantage later on. The north's supra regional interest factor in the passage of the bill collapsed soon after when the President refused assent for it, bringing to the foreground the regionalist character of the struggle for resources.

It follows that it is the interests of regions, as distinct from the interests of individuals or classes that are doubtless bound up with them, that are in contention and are the forces that shape the principles of revenue allocation and federal government expenditure in Nigeria. Thus, individual and class interests mesh within regional interests in regard to federal resource allocation. Individual interests may not always feed regional interests. This does not by itself suggest that they do not count in the region as a whole. If they are viewed by the people of a region as such (strictly as individual interests), then Nigeria can lay claim to a high level of class consciousness. However in Nigeria, where the bourgeois class is fractionalized, individuals cannot, even for their own self interests, not bother about group interests since group interests always hold the prospect of feeding individual interests. Hence, the contention over resources in Nigeria is not usually between classes or interest groups as such but between ethnic/regional groups. The national image that such cross-regional lobby coalitions as the Governors' Forum, Chairmen of Local Governments' Forum and Speakers' Forum under the current democratic dispensation could cut for themselves is soon shattered by the activities of sectional groupings.

The centralization of resources is not simply for the benefit of the Nigerian bourgeoisie although they have benefited more. It has been fostered by the dominant ethnic/regional groups for the benefit of all their peoples though inequitably distributed between the bourgeoisie and the rest of the populace. Individuals may make claims to resources in the name of their group in the calculation that they will get more for themselves if they succeed. Yet, because of the coupling in Nigeria of pluralist political organization and the communal character of being Africans, as Ake (1994) has argued: they will measure their share of collective wealth in terms of their group's share. Hence, apparently comfortable individuals who have used public office to acquire immense wealth are heard to bemoan their group's disadvantage in the distribution of resources in Nigeria. In the context of regional competition for resources, then, the ethnic composition of vital government structures such as the powerful presidency has become of vital interest to ethno-regional groups.

## Note

1. Professor Olugbemiro Jegede, Vice-Chancellor, National Open University of Nigeria in a presentation to the 19 Northern Governors' Forum, *The Guardian*, Lagos, March 1, 2005, p. 5. Details of more elaborate statistical evidence are provided in Chapter Four.

## References

Abernethy, D. B., 1969, *The Political Dilemma of Popular Education: An African Case*, Stanford: The University Press.

Aboyade, O., 1983, *Integrated Economics – A Study of Developing Economies,* London: Addison-Wesley Publishers.

Adedeji, A., 1969, *Nigeria Federal Finance*, London: Hunchinson Educational.

Ake, C., 1994, *Democratization of Disempowerment in Africa*, Lagos: Malthouse.

Akinyele, R. T., 2004, 'Ethnicity, Religion and Politics in Nigeria', in Richard A. Olaniyan ed., *The Amalgamation and its Enemies: An Interpretive History of Modern Nigeria,* Ile-Ife: Obafemi Awolowo University Press Limited, pp. 123-147.

Alli, M. C., 2004, *The Federal Republic of Nigerian Army*, Lagos: Malthouse.

Ayodele, O. S., Egwaikhide, F. O., Isumonah, V. A. and Oyeranti, O. A., 2005, in 'Supreme Court Judgement and Aftermaths', in Akinola A. Owosekun, Ode Ojowu & Festus O. Egwaikhide eds., *Contemporary Issues in the Management of the Nigerian Economy,* Ibadan: NISER, pp. 361-382.

Bienen, H., 1981, 'The Politics of Income Distribution: Institutions, Class, and Ethnicity' in H. Bienen and V. P. Diejomaoh, eds., *The Political Economy of Income Distribution in Nigeria,* New York, London: Holmes and Meier Publishers, Inc.

Bienen, H., 1983, 'The State and Ethnicity: Integrative Formulas in Africa', in D. Rothchild and V. Olorunsola, eds., *State Versus Ethnic Claims: African Policy Dilemmas*, Boulder, Colorado: Westview Press, pp. 100-125.

Chabal, P. and Daloz, J.-P. , 1999, *Africa Works: Disorder as Political Instrument,* Oxford: James Currey and Bloomington & Indianapolis: Indiana University Press.

Bates, R. H., 1974, 'Ethnic Competition and Modernization in Contemporary Africa', *Comparative Political Studies*, Vol. 6, No. 4, pp. 457-484.

Dahrendorf, R., 1988, *The Modern Social Conflict: An Essay on the Politics of Liberty*, Berkeley, Los Angeles: University of California Press.

Conlan, T., 1998, *From New Federalism to Devolution: Twenty-five Years of Intergovernmental Reform*, Washington, D.C.: Brookings Institution Press.

Diamond, L., 1987, 'Class Formation in the Swollen African State', *Journal of Modern African Studies*, Vol. 24, No. 4, pp. 567-596.

Ekeh, P. P., 1975, 'Colonialism and the Two Publics in Africa: A Theoretical Statement', *Comparative Studies in Society and History*, Vol. 17, pp. 91-112.

Ekeh, Peter, P., 2000, 'Nigerian Political History and the Foundations of Nigerian Federalism', *Annals of the Social Science Academy of Nigeria*, No. 12, pp. 1-16.

Elazar, D. J., 1987, *Exploring Federalism*, Tuscaloosa, AL: University of Alabama Press.

Forrest, T., 1995, *Politics and Economic Development in Nigeria*, Boulder, Colorado: Westview Press.

Gana, A. T., 'Federalism and the National Question in Nigeria: A Theoretical Exploration,' in Aaron T. Gana and Samuel G. Egwu, eds., 2003, *Federalism in Africa Vol.1: Framing the National Question*, Trenton, NJ and Asmara, Eritrea: Africa World Press, Inc., pp. 143-160.

Graf, W. D., 1979, *Elections 1979- The Nigerian Citizen's Guide to Parties, Politics, Leaders and Issues*, Lagos: Daily Times.

Gurr, T. R., 1993, *Minorities at Risk: A Global View of Ethnopolitical Conflicts*, United States Institute of Peace, Washington DC.

Hoetink, H., 1975, 'Resource Competition, Monopoly, and Socio-racial Diversity', in Leo A. Despres, ed., *Ethnicity and Resource Competition in Plural Societies*, New York: Mouton Publishers, pp. 9-25.

Ikime, O., 'The Nigerian Civil War and the National Question: A Historical Analysis', in Eghosa E. Osaghae, E. Nwudiwe & R.T. Suberu, eds., 2002, *The Civil War and Aftermath*, Ibadan: Program on Ethnic and Federal Studies, pp. 52-73.

Isumonah, V. A., 2003, 'Land Tenure, Migration, Citizenship and Communal Conflicts in Africa', *Nationalism and Ethnic Politics*, Vol. 9, No.1, Spring, pp. 1-19.

Isumonah, V. A., 2004, 'The Making of the Ogoni Ethnic Group', *Africa: Journal of the International African Institute*, London, Vol. 74, No. 3, pp. 433-453.

Isumonah, V. A. and Egwaikhide, F. O., 2005, 'The Use of Agencies in Ethno-regional Struggle for Resources in Nigeria', *African Journal of Political Science*.

Jinadu, L. A., 2002, *Ethnic Conflicts and Federalism in Nigeria*, No. 49, ZEF –Discussion Papers on Development, Bonn.

Joseph, R. A., 1981, 'Democratization under Military Tutelage: Crisis and Consensus in the Nigerian 1979 Elections', *Comparative Politics*, pp. 75-100.

Joseph, R. A., 1983, 'Class, State, and Prebendal Politics in Nigeria', *Journal of Commonwealth and Comparative Politics*, Vol. 21, No. 3, pp. 21-37.

Joseph, R. A., 1987, *Democracy and Prebendal Politics in Nigeria: The Rise and Fall of the Second Republic*, Cambridge University Press.

Kasfir, N., 1983, 'Relating Class to State in Africa', *The Journal of Commonwealth and Comparative Politics*, Vol. 21, No. 3, pp. 1-20.

Lewis, P., 1996, 'From Prebendalism to Predation: the Political Economy of Decline in Nigeria', *The Journal of Modern African Studies*, Vol. 34, No. 1, pp. 79-103.

Maiz, R., 2003, 'Politics and Nation: Nationalist Mobilization of Ethnic Differences' *Nations and Nationalism*, Vol. 9, No. 2, pp. 195-212.

Mamdani, M., 2000, 'Beyond Settler and Native as Political Identities: Overcoming the Political Legacy of Colonialism' in Centre for Advanced Social Science (CASS), *Ideology and African Development, Proceedings of the Third Memorial Programme in Honour of Professor Claude Ake*, Port Harcourt: CASS, pp. 4-22.

Mbanefoh, G. F., 1986, 'Military Presence and the Future of Nigerian Fiscal Federalism', *Faculty of the Social Sciences Lecture Series*, No.1 (University of Ibadan).

Moore, M., 2004, 'Revenues, State Formation, and the Quality of Governance in Developing Countries', *International Political Science Review*, Vol. 25, ,No. 3, pp. 297-319.

Moynihan, D. P., 1979, 'Patterns of Ethnic Succession: Blacks and Hispanics in New York City', *Political Science Quarterly*, Vol. 94, No. 1, pp. 1-14.

Musgrave, R. A., 1969, 'Theories of Federalism', *Public Finance*, Vol. 24, pp. 521-532.

Nandy, A., 1988, 'Introduction: Science as a Reason of the State', in Nandy ed., *Science, Hegemony and Violence: A Requiem for Modernity*, Tokyo: The UN University & Delhi: Oxford University Press, pp. 1-23.

Nathan, R. P. and Hoffmann, E. P., 1991, 'Modern Federalism', *International Affairs*, pp. 27-38.

Nnoli, O., 1980, *Ethnic Politics in Nigeria*, Enugu: Fourth Dimension Press.

Ogbuagu, C. S. A., 1985, 'The Politics of Industrial Location in Nigeria', *Africa Development*, Vol. 10, No. 1, pp. 97-122.

Onyeoziri, F., 2002, 'Conceptualizing the National Question', in E. Osaghae and Ebere Onwudiwe, eds., *The Management of the National Question in Nigeria*, Ibadan: Programme on Ethnic and Federal Studies, pp. 35-48.

Otite, O., 1990, *Ethnic Pluralism and Ethnicity in Nigeria (with Comparative Materials)*, Ibadan: Shaneson C.I. Ltd.

Oyovbaire, S. E., 1985, *Federalism in Nigeria: A Study in the Development of the Nigerian State*, London: Macmillan Publishers.

Premdas, R. R., 1995, *Ethnic Conflict and Development: Case of Guyana*, Aldershot: Avebury.

Reno, W., 1993, 'Old Brigades, Money Bags, New Breeds and the Ironies of Reform in Nigeria', *Canadian Journal of African Studies*, Vol. 27, No. 1, pp. 65-87.

Rupley, L., 1981, 'Revenue Sharing in the Nigerian Federation', *The Journal of Modern African Studies*, Vol. 19, No. 2, pp. 258-277.

Salamone, F. A., 1975, 'Becoming Hausa: Ethnic Identity Change and its Implications for the Study of Ethnic Pluralism and Stratification', *Africa*, Vol. 45, No. 4, pp. 410-423.

Schwarz, W., 1968, *Nigeria*, London: Pall Mall Press, 1968.

Stolper, W. F., 1970, 'Some Considerations Concerning the Allocation of Fiscal Resources', *The Quarterly Journal of Administration*, Vol. 5, No. 2, pp. 83-91.

Suberu, R. T., 1991, *State and Local Government Reorganizations in Nigeria*, Ibadan: IFRA, 1994.

Takaya, B. J., 'Socio-political Forces in the Evolution and Consolidation of the Kaduna Mafia' in B. J. Takaya and S. G. Tyoden, eds., 1987, *The Kaduna Mafia*, Jos: Jos University Press Ltd., pp. 29-45.

Tanzi, V., 1996, 'Fiscal Federalism and Decentralization: A Review of Some Efficiency and Macroeconomic Aspects in 1996' The International Bank for Reconstruction and Development/The World Bank Report, Washington, D.C., pp. 295-316.

Tobi, D., 1989, 'Inter-governmental Fiscal Relations and the Public Policy Process in Nigeria', in Alex Gboyega, et. al. eds., *Nigeria Since Independence, The First 25 Years, Volume VIII: Public Administration*, Heinemann Educational Books (Nigeria) Limited, pp. 126-158.

Turner, T., 1978, 'Commercial Capitalism and the 1975 Coup', in Keith Pater-Brick, ed., *Soldiers and Oil: the Political Transformation of Nigeria*, London, pp. 166-197.

Ukwu, I. U., 1987, 'Federal Financing of Projects for National Development and integration', in Ukwu, I. Ukwu, ed., *Federal Character and National Integration in Nigeria*, Kuru, Jos: National Institute for Policy and Strategic Studies, pp. 113-129.

Wibbels, E., 2003, 'Bailouts, Budget Constraints and Leviathans: Comparative Federalism and Lessons from the Early United States', *Comparative Political Studies*, Vol. 36, No. 5, pp. 475-508.

Williams, G., 1980, *State and Society in Nigeria*, Idanre: Afrografika Publishers.

Young, C., 1976, *The Politics of Cultural Pluralism*, Madison: University of Wisconsin Press.

# 3

## Fiscal History

The political unification of the north and south in 1914 and the constitutional developments thereafter brought the issue of inter-governmental fiscal relations to the fore in Nigeria. One main problem was how to share revenue between the regions. The derivation principle dominated interregional revenue allocation between the late 1940s and the mid-1960s. As oil revenue-dominated public finance following the Middle East crisis of 1973-74, the derivation principle was de-emphasized. Simultaneously, population and equality of states criteria were emphasized to the fullest degree possible. These principles did and still do not favour the oil-producing region of Nigeria today. Also, how to share revenue among the three levels of government featured prominently. The various military regimes exercised the power of veto on fiscal matters. All these fuelled the petulant struggle among the regions for the control of political power at the centre for eventual resource allocation. This chapter is a brief history of the allocation arrangements in Nigeria.

### Vertical Revenue Allocation

The struggle for revenue allocation takes place between the centre and sub-national governments under the label of vertical revenue allocation. Several plausible factors account for this. A prime consideration is the existence of a vertical fiscal gap, a situation in which there is a discrepancy between the constitutionally assigned functions and the taxing power – sometimes dubbed the non-correspondence problem. Vertical competition for financial resources has also been explained in terms of competition between members of the bourgeois class who control political power at the federal level and those that exert political influence at the local level (see Adebayo 1990). To a large extent, such a striving for resources is trans-ethnic and trans-regional. In most cases, vertical fiscal balance favours central government.

#### Revenue Transferred from Federal to Sub-national Levels

Where transfers to lower levels of government are inadequate to carry out their functions, there will be agitation for revenue-sharing arrangements that would strengthen the fiscal position of regional and local units. Failure to design an appropriate vertical revenue-sharing formula to reflect the constitutionally assigned functions is expected to provoke inter-governmental fiscal conflict. Thus, the desperate bid to generate more revenue to carry out their activities may precipitate the imposition of multiple taxation, charges and levies at the state and local levels. Such unjustifiable and unco-ordinated multiple taxation makes it exceedingly difficult, even impossible, to achieve optimal fiscal arrangements and distorts efficient resource allocation. Mbanefoh (1993) identifies four important phases of inter-tier revenue allocation in Nigeria. First is the period between 1946 and 1951 during which the federal government exercised overwhelming control over the revenue it collected. During this period, the sharing of revenue between the federal government and regional government was not formalized. Revenue allo-cation to the regions was at the discretion of the federal government. The second phase, between 1952 and 1966, witnessed the formal sharing of revenue between the federal and regional governments. With the military intervention in Nigerian politics in 1966, the federal government increasingly appropriated more of the centrally collected revenue. This tendency that lasted till 1976 is what Mbanefoh (1993) classified as the third stage. The fourth and last period is the era of inter-governmental fiscal tension that commenced in the early 1980s. Mbanefoh did not explicate the nature and causes of the inter-governmental fiscal conflict.

While it may be difficult to disagree with the classifications presented by Mbanefoh, some comments are desirable. It is the increasing process of concen-tration that has deprived the sub-national governments of their legitimate reve-nue. Fiscal centralization has led to the conclusion that the federal government is superior to the other two layers of government. Yet, under federalism, the different layers of government are necessarily co-ordinate with each exerting direct in-fluence on the people. Also, inter-governmental fiscal conflict intensified partly because the scope of governmental activities vastly expanded at the state-local level with the oil boom in the 1970s and the traditional sources of revenue becoming grossly inadequate for states and local governments to provide public services to the desired level.

### Horizontal Revenue Allocation

Horizontal revenue allocation has to do with the sharing of the consolidated revenue allocated to states or local governments from the Federation Account between the states or local governments. Several principles have been applied from the late 1940s. A principle that has featured prominently is derivation. The Phillipson fiscal commission (Phillipson 1948) first recommended it and the fiscal commissions that followed (e.g. Hicks and Phillipson 1951; Chicks 1954; and Raiseman and Tress 1958) recommended derivation, but in varying degrees. According to this principle, each region should receive a proportion of revenue it contributes to the centrally collected revenue. The Phillipson Commission reasoned that this principle would enable each region to align its expenditure with the available revenue. Thus, derivation stresses fiscal discipline. There was a second reason for recommending the derivation principle. It was thought that regional governments would have substantial autonomy over time. For these reasons, it can be argued that derivation was not only right-thinking but also desirable. The Phillipson Commission acknowledged that derivation could make the rich regions richer and the poor regions poorer. Even then, it was noted that the overall benefits of derivation outweighed the disadvantages.

Derivation was used to the fullest degree possible in the allocation of revenue between the regions. The regional distribution of the consumption of imported items, on which duties were imposed and that also formed the basis for derivation, had to be based largely on broad assumptions and approximations for lack of accurate statistical data. Thus, calculations based on such assumptions were subject to wide margins of errors and could not be relied upon for revenue allocation. Insistent use of the derivation principle for revenue sharing thus negated the equity and fairness that inspired it. Derivation was also criticized for being a source of inter-regional conflict, rivalry and antagonism. This is because it promoted uneven development. It was common for regions not favoured by it to oppose its use.

Statistics on the regional distribution of revenue for the period 1953-1965 show wide spatial variations. The share of the Northern region of the total revenue remained relatively stable in the thirteen years, averaging about 33 per cent annually. Comparatively, the mean share of the Western region was 40 per cent, while the balance went to the Eastern Region. The situation changed from the 1970s onwards. For instance, the share of the Northern region was highest at about 38 per cent in 1970/74 with the Eastern region following with 24 per cent. The Western region got 23 per cent and the Mid-western region received 15 per cent.

As oil revenue began to dominate Nigeria's public finance, the importance of the derivation principle started to fade. Oil revenue grew astronomically in the early 1970s because of the Middle East crisis in 1973-74, together with the various petroleum tax reforms implemented by the central government. Such a huge rise in oil revenue fuelled the strident struggle for revenue allocation among the regions. A 1987 federal government report (The Political Bureau 1987) suggests that there is a direct relationship between the control of economic resources and political power in Nigeria. If that is correct, the significant use of derivation would have made the oil-producing region economically strong and politically powerful. The dominant majority whose interest in oil revenue has exacerbated regional competition for oil rents could not countenance this.

An intellectual aspect of the distributional coalition/struggle for oil revenues should be noted. According to Adebayo (1990), members of the 'Ibadan School' (used in two senses – 'locational' and generic) argued persuasively that derivation should be given less emphasis, in part because it is rooted in a weak theoretical foundation. Take a few examples. The Technical Committee on Revenue Allocation, headed by Professor Ojetunji Aboyade did not recommend the derivation principle as a basis for inter-regional revenue allocation. Also, the report of the Presidential Commission on Revenue Allocation Volume IV contains the views of the minority report in which Prof. Dotun Phillips, a member of the Ibadan School, argued indefatigably that the government should move away from derivation that tends to be export-oriented and dependent on the vagaries of international market. Some of the proposals of the Ibadan School undoubtedly facilitated the dropping of the derivation principle.

The views of the Ibadan School have been criticized for being too economistic, ignoring the fact that fiscal federalism is in the domain of economics of politics. The argument that derivation would accelerate uneven development is unfounded and baseless. Unequal fiscal capacity, that is, the uneven distribution of revenue collection and expenditure needs between sub-national units is the natural fallout of fiscal decentralization, the essence of the federal system of government not opposed by the Ibadan School. It follows that more services will be provided in states or regions that are relatively wealthier. The literature on fiscal decentralization indicates that the solution to the unequal fiscal-capacity problem lies in the grant system.

Even the argument that derivation breeds regional conflicts and hostility is refutable (Mbanefoh and Egwaikhide 1998). As the Ibadan School argues, the elimination of the derivation principle would foster and reinforce unity and also engender development. What is the evidence? Inter-regional rivalry and hostility deepened between the mid-1960s and 1999 when the derivation principle paled into insignificance.

As derivation became less significant, two principles – population and equality of states – became prominent. A weight of 40 per cent was initially attached to population. This was later reduced to 30 per cent. Population is a surrogate for need. The basic logic here is: the use of population rests on the notion that development must be people-centred. However, the crude application of this principle has made it objectionable. Only total population is considered. Nevertheless, demographic characteristics of the population should be more relevant since they directly influence the tax base and the expenditure needs of the different regions. Hence, Phillips (1975) proposed actual expenditure obligation of states as the basis for sharing revenue. That, to some extent, reflects the need which population tends to measure. He re-echoed the advantages of this extensively in his minority report five years later.

It is generally acknowledged that the use of population in its crudest form has made it exceedingly difficult to have accurate and reliable census figures. Population was one major factor explored to create more states and local government councils from the existing ones in the past and has been used inappropriately for revenue allocation. Under the current horizontal revenue allocation, the states of Kano and Lagos benefit immensely from the use of population.

For the purposes of revenue allocation, the demographic features of the population are more useful than the total population. Even if demographic characteristics of the population were to be considered, the relevant statistics are hard to find. The resolution of the demographic variables does not make population a valuable criterion for revenue allocation. Perhaps an example will throw more light on this. Suppose there are two states with the same population. In one of the states, per capita income is at the subsistence level, but income is fairly evenly distributed. In the second state, income is highly unevenly distributed and the poor in this state have access to basic needs since most people have control over economic resources (Due and Friedlaender 1977:107). The needs of this state are expected to be significantly different from those of the first even though they both have the same population. In this respect, the use of aggregate population as a basis for revenue allocation, presumably because it reflects need, is simply misleading.

Next is the equality of states principle. This principle attracts a weight of 40 per cent. The implication of this is that 40 per cent of the revenue allocated to all the states from the Federation Account is shared equally between the states. Findings have revealed that the total revenue allocated to all the states and the Federal Capital Territory (FCT) in any given year, based on this principle, usually exceeds the combined internally generated revenue of all the states by more than a factor of two. Statistics also show that the Northern states benefit more from the equality of states in horizontal revenue allocation. Another informative insight is that the equality of state-based revenue accounts for more than one-third of the total recurrent expenditure of all the states and FCT. Its contribution to some states is significantly above this average. From this principle of equality, states that were split receive more from.

Equality of states means equal shares for each of the states in the Nigerian federation. This principle does not take account the differences in population, fiscal capacity of states and other resource endowments. Available data for the fiscal year 2001 indicated that the internally generated revenue of Lagos state was N12.5 billion. This figure is more than the total expenditure of sixteen states, confirming that states in Nigeria are not equal economically. By implication, the budgetary obligations, or better still, the developmental goals of one state would vary significantly from the other and through time (Phillips 1975 has provided some of these highlights). Perhaps, the principle of equality of states can be interpreted to mean that each sub-national unit is expected to carry out minimum statutory functions. Even though states may have the same number of institutions, the personnel involved (and therefore cost) may be different, as is actually the case in Nigeria.

Phillips, in his minority report contained in Volume 5 of the Okigbo *Report of the Revenue Allocation Commission of 1980*, calculated the principle each of the states relied on most of the period, which was 1978-79. His findings showed that eight of the nineteen states of the federation depended on population most; and of the eight states, four were from the north, three from the southeast and the remaining one from the southwest. Only two states (Bendel, which now comprises Edo and Delta; and Rivers, now bifurcated into Rivers and Bayelsa states) were found to have relied most on the derivation principle. The remaining nine states leaned heavily on the equality of states principle. Further examination reveals that these criteria – population and equality of states – favour states of the dominant ethnic groups. This in part explains why, in spite of the various criticisms leveled against these principles, they are still in use and the weights attached are still substantial. Politically, it also explains why any proposal to emphasize derivation with a large weight has very little probability of being passed and confirms the point of the Political Bureau that there is a strong relationship between the use of derivation and control of political power.

Landmass and terrain is a relatively recent principle. The historical development of this criterion is well documented by Mbanefoh (1993) and some of the problems associated with it noted by Emenuga (1993:98). More states in the north generally supported this principle than southern states. Probably because it favours the regions that control political power for a long time, land mass and terrain was quietly introduced without subjecting it to public debate.

**Fiscal Centralization**

A striking feature of Nigeria's fiscal federalism is increased fiscal centralization. Perhaps this draws from the aspects of the Wiseman-Peacock hypothesis that as the economy grows, the central government's role increases. The concentration process is central to Mbanefoh's (1986) Faculty of the Social Sciences Lecture series of the University of Ibadan, Nigeria. He argued that following military intervention in Nigerian politics, the federal government assumed responsibility for the provision of goods and services that were hitherto the responsibility of states. The promulgation of Decrees Nos. 13 and 9, in 1970 and 1971 respectively, enhanced the fiscal centralization of the federal government. The military government exercised the power of veto in the allocation of revenue. Given its command and hierarchical structure, the superiority of the federal government in its relationship with the states was particularly evident. Thus, the federal government appropriated a sizeable proportion of the Federation Account. Obsessed with power, the federal military government arbitrarily aggregated functions that should not normally be within its purview, according to Buchana's efficiency and geographic range of spill-over effect principles in the allocation functions. The establishment of special accounts – the Stabilization Fund, Dedicated Accounts, and the Petroleum Trust Fund (PTF) – exacerbated fiscal concentration in Nigeria. The funds paid into these accounts were federally collected and should have been paid into the Federation Account for vertical allocation among the three levels of government.

In addition to these, several deductions were made from the Federation Account before the balance was shared. In this respect, there is the first line charge created by the federal government in its budget. The elements considered under this budget items are external debt service payments, joint venture contracts, the NNPC priority projects, national priority projects and funding of the judiciary. These are charged to the Federation Account Funds because all the items are deducted from the Federation Account before the balance is shared between the three tiers of government. A direct result of this is inter-governmental fiscal conflict. When this action was challenged, the Supreme Court of Nigeria declared this practice of the federal government unconstitutional (Ayodele, Egwaikhide, Isumonah & Oyeranti 2005).

## Special Issues

A major special issue that has occupied the centre stage since the mid-1970s is the environmental effects of oil production. The Okigbo Fiscal Commission acknowledged this and recommended that a certain percentage of the revenue in the Federation Account should be paid into the Special Funds to address the problems of oil-producing areas, together with ecological and related problems. It is now known that the negative externalities in the oil-producing areas are substantial. Hutchful (1970) was one of the very first to comprehensively docu- ment the environmental pollution associated with oil production in the Niger Delta. Oil production pollution in the Niger Delta takes different forms. The generally reported sources of negative externalities include seismic surveys, canalization, poor waste disposal, oil spillage and gas flaring (see *Newswatch*, January 8, 1996, Special Report). Perhaps oil spillage and gas flaring are the more common and significant sources that are reported. In an authoritative study, Awobajo (1981) reports that between 1976 and 1980 a total of 784 spills involving about 1.34 million barrels of crude oil occurred in Nigeria. For the period between 1976 and 1990, the World Bank estimates put the figure at 2.1 million barrels of crude oil in 2,796 incidents (reported in *Newswatch*, January 8 1996 and *Tell*, December 18, 1995, p. 18). The externalities have adversely affected man and human activities in the oil-bearing communities. Indeed, the destruction of the space-economy and aquatic life has generated tension, protest and ever-increasing debate in recent years.

At the analytical level, Stewart and Ghani (1991) have argued that the evaluation of externalities and the decision whether or not to take action are influenced by the category of agents involved – that is, small or large, poor or rich, etc. The hypothesis here is that when externalities affect a small and politically un-influential group they will be undervalued in comparison with those affecting the big, rich and powerful groups. It follows that effective ameliorative measures would be pursued when the externalities affect members of the influential class or a large ethnic group.

In 1981, the federal government approved 1.5 per cent of the total revenue in the Federation Account for the development of oil-producing areas. The funds accumulated in the vaults of the Central Bank of Nigeria (CBN) until 1990 when a task force was set up to administer the money. As has been pointed out, the decision to use the fund was apparently a swift reaction to an unsuccessful military *coup* to oust the Babangida military administration. Major Gideon Orkar, who led the 1990 *coup* and his colleagues, mostly of Niger Delta origin, accused the federal government of not developing oil-producing areas. A direct translation of the allegations by those carrying out the *coup* is nothing but an inadequate federal presence in spite of the fact that the bulk of the financial resources of Nigeria comes from oil-producing areas.

However in 1992 the federal military government established the Oil Mineral Producing Areas Developing Commission (OMPADEC) to superintend the 1.5 per cent (later raised to 3 per cent) allocation from the Federation Account for the development of the oil-producing areas. Simultaneously, the government instructed each of the oil-producing firms to spend 5 per cent of its annual budget in executing development programmes in the region or states in which they operate.

OMPADEC did not meet the aspirations of the oil-producing areas. Two major hypotheses are offered for the poor performance of the commission. First, OMPADEC was grossly under-funded. In the period 1993-97, it received a cumulative amount of N11 billion. Of course, this was a far cry from the statutory 3 per cent of the Federation Account approved for this agency. Second, OMPADEC was riddled with a political power game of control between the oil-producing states, on the one hand, and between the oil-producing states and the federal government, on the other. The Head of State and Commander-in-Chief of the Armed Forces had overwhelming influence on the day-to-day operations of OMPADEC since he had the power to appoint and fire the chairperson of OMPADEC and its commissioners. Indeed, the decree establishing the commission vested too much power on its chairperson who was directly responsible to the president. There was hardly any correlation between the oil production quota of the oil-producing states and the projects executed by the commission. Yet the decree establishing OMPADEC specified that the value of projects must reflect the oil production from the state. Thus, it is difficult to conclude that OMPADEC maintained neutrality and equity in its activities.

A third hypothesis is that OMPADEC did not perform because of corruption. A revealing testimony of this was the indiscriminate award of contracts by OMPADEC management. The interim report of the Alhaji Inuwa investigation panel that appraised failed and non-performing federal contracts showed 1,117 uncompleted projects across the eight oil-producing states (see *Sunday Punch*, October 24, 1999, p. 3). The bureau was sternly criticized from within and outside the oil-producing states for lack of expenditure control and gross lack of financial transparency and accountability. Consistent with this is the allegation that OMPADEC was used to settle vociferous citizens in the oil-producing areas (See *Tell*, Lagos, December 18, 1995, pp. 16-17). By Decree 51 of 1969 and pursuant to Section 40(3) of the 1979 Constitution, the ownership and control of petroleum in Nigeria is vested in the federal government. While crude oil remains a common resource, the environmental pollution is borne solely by the oil-producing areas. Based on the taxonomy of externalities from the relatively very recent literature, it can be argued that those oil production activities are largely either producer-producer or producer-consumer types, and the number of interacting agents are of many variety (this conclusion is derived from Stewart and Ghani's 1991 discussion of different externalities).

Egwaikhide and Aregbeyen (1999) have suggested that, in line with the literature, the oil firms responsible for the environmental pollution in the Niger Delta should be made to pay tax. In an economic sense, pollution is a commodity that currently attracts a zero price. Users of the goods and services produced by the oil firms would bear the burden of the tax in the form of higher prices. The revenue collected from such a tax could be used to compensate the oil communities that are adversely affected by pollution. Imposition of a tax would hopefully compel oil firms to take measures to control and manage the negative spill-over effects of their production activities.

## The Demand for Resource Control

Nigeria returned to civil rule on May 29, 1999 after several years of military dictatorship. This offered individuals and groups the opportunity to vent their anger without any fear of molestation and intimidation. Buoyed by this development, the youth, under different labels (e.g. the Egbesu Boys), of the oil-producing communities intensified the demand for a fair share of oil revenue. Strategies employed by the youths included frequent attacks on oil installations, bursting of oil pipes and holding of oil workers hostage. Leaders of oil-producing states were of the view that the introduction of the onshore/off-shore dichotomy in the allocation of oil revenue by the Obasanjo-led civilian administration amounted to a continuation of the politics of hatred and marginalization of oil-producing ethnic minorities. It was felt that the negative externalities associated with oil production make it particularly imperative for the derivation principle to be used to the fullest degree possible, as was the case in the 1950s and 1960s. The people of the oil-producing states have repeatedly cited the case of the marble mining at Igbeti in Oyo State (Yoruba West of Nigeria) where the state government takes 30 per cent of the mining royalties, the local government of extraction takes 10 per cent and the Igbeti community 15 per cent. The remainder is shared between the marble company (25 per cent) and the federal government (20 per cent). Also, derivation was not fully applied by the federal government since it excluded gas. For these reasons, the federal government was accused of double standards in the application of derivation. All this precipitated and remains as fuel for widespread and deep-rooted agitation for resource control.

The demand for resource control was given a fresh impetus at the periodic meeting of the seventeen southern governors beginning in 2000. All southern governors appeared to have supported resource control. They generally acknowledged that the fiscal issue constitutes the lifeblood of federalism. Therefore, it was posited that three principles – national interest, need and derivation - must be considered in the inter-regional sharing of revenue. Other fiscal matters were raised at the forum of the southern governors. An important one was the payment of primary school teachers' salaries.

Universal Basic Education (UBE) is one of the cardinal programmes of the PDP-controlled federal government. In pursuing the implementation of UBE, the federal government peremptorily expanded the scope of its responsibilities. Given that Nigeria is now under civil rule, this should have been an issue for constitutional debate and review. Arbitrary deductions of revenue meant for local governments from the Federation Account hinder the promotion of local democracy and democratic consolidation (Norregaard 1995). The federal government knows full well that irregular or non-payment of salaries of primary school teachers would inhibit the effective delivery of the UBE programme. To avoid this problem, the federal government decided to deduct (every month) a huge amount of money directly from the revenue allocated to local governments from the Federation Account. In consequence, many local governments were left with little revenue from the Federation Account. Many of them faced fiscal crisis since revenue from the Federation Account is the only major source of revenue for local governments. This is what gave rise to the label *zero allocation*.

The deductions from the Federation Account for the payment of teachers' salaries were repugnant to all thirty-six state governors. Indeed, the state governors argued that it was not appropriate for the federal government to make the deductions and administer the funds without the authorization of the state governments. This is because the 1999 Constitution of the Federal Republic of Nigeria says that primary education is the responsibility of the state government, and that local government only participates with the state government. This was an important issue brought before the Supreme Court for it to pass judgment on.

The north is generally opposed to resource control. It opined that resource control would cause chaos and political instability. According to northern leaders, resource control would make states too strong to be tempted to declare political independence. Thus, they have considered it a euphemism for confederation and the subsequent disintegration of Nigeria. For these reasons, northern leaders continue to advocate a strong central government. This position is not entirely new, for this agenda was vigorously pursued by successive military regimes controlled by the north. Currently, the bulk of the federally collected revenue is dominated by oil produced from the south. It is not surprising that resource control is unacceptable to the north since it will reduce its revenue from the Federation

Account and threaten its long-term financial survival. It will be recalled that, before the amalgamation of the north and south in 1914, the former ran huge persistent budget deficits while the latter recorded surpluses. The north has, as expected, not supported resource control that may reduce its share from the Federation Account since the current fiscal arrangement is favourable to it.

During the resource control controversy, the north vehemently argued that it was not fair for the oil-producing states to enjoy both the 13 per cent derivation revenue and the Niger Development Commission (NDDC). In this regard, they made reference to the Shiroro dam that provides hydropower to the country. They called for adequate compensation and demanded the establishment of the Hydropower Electric Power Areas Development Commission (HYPARDEC) by the federal government since electricity from this source is considered vital to Nigeria's economic development. In 2001, this issue produced rowdy sessions in the lower house of the National Assembly. The eastern leaders were on their part hoping for the establishment of the Erosion Development Commission (ERODEC) that will cater for the devastating effects of erosion. The north had its way in May 2003 when the federal lawmakers eventually passed a bill establishing HYPARDEC after the general elections.

Another important concern to all the state governors was the *first line charge* of the federal government. The key elements of this in the federal government's budget are external debt service payments, joint venture contracts and the Nigeria National Petroleum Corporation (NNPC) priority projects. The funds for these items are usually deducted from the Federation Account before the balance is shared between the three levels of government. State governments raised an objection to this practice because it is not backed by the constitution and the fact that it reduces the revenue in the Federation Account for vertical allocation. The feeling was that the federal government should service its debt from its own revenue and not from the Federation Account.

Similarly, the states accused the federal government of unilaterally withholding part of the revenue meant for the Federation Account. For instance, the fiscal year 2000 witnessed rapid growth in revenue from increased prices of crude oil in the world market. About N198 billon (about US$1.8.0 billion) was paid into a stabilization account, perhaps unknown to state governments, by the federal government. This decision was influenced by the need to maintain macro-economic stability since the stabilization policy is the responsibility of the federal government. The CBN defended the action of the federal government on the grounds that the sharing of the excess crude oil revenue would boost domestic liquidity, expand money growth, fuel price inflation and weaken the exchange rate. As logical as this may be, state governors (with Governor Olusegun Osoba of Ogun State as the most vociferous) challenged the federal government that there was no basis in law for not declaring the revenue for allocation. Arising from this was the issue of transparency and accountability on the part of the federal government in respect of the revenue collected into the Federation Account. Sustained pressure from the governors forced the federal government to release the funds for sharing between the tiers of government. Thereafter, the state governors demanded that the federal government render account of the revenue collected on a regular basis. In order to control the excess liquidity arising from this, the CBN issued certificates, a money market instrument, with attractive interest rates. Statistics show that a total amount of N256 billion was offered by the CBN in 2001.

Next is the inequitable federal presence. Federal finance (which usually takes the form of transfers, grants, purchases, taxes and expenditures) has a direct impact, with multiplier effects, on the economies of sub-national governments. In particular, federal expenditure in a region (or state) directly affects employment, output and income (Musgrave and Musgrave 1980). Thus, a federal presence influences resource allocation and regional development. The last military regimes (those of Generals Ibrahim Babagida and Sani Abacha) gave rise to new forms of distributional coalitions that manifested in the establishment of special accounts and programmes. Such accounts included the Stabilization Fund, Dedicated Accounts and the Petroleum Trust Fund (PTF); while some of the special programmes were: the National Directorate of Employment (NDE); Directorate of Food, Roads and Rural Infrastructure (DEFRI); the Better Life Programme (BLP); and the Family Economic Advancement Programme (FEAP). In general, these programmes unjustifiably favoured the north more than the south. This provoked the call by southern leaders for a restructured federal system that would have a weak centre. Of course, the north opposed this.

The federal government, on the other hand, maintained that the natural resources located in the continental shelf of Nigeria do not belong to any state but itself. These contrasting situations point to the fact that federalism is characterized by the interplay of political power struggle between the various interest groups in the federation. There are those who favour fiscal centralization from this analysis (the north) or decentralization (the south) because it serves their economic and political interests. Explicit from the debates is the primacy of fiscal bargaining as the nucleus of federalism.

### Effects of the Supreme Court Judgment

The judgment of the Supreme Court has far-reaching implications for all levels of government in Nigeria. The Supreme Court's decision threw the federal government's budget for the fiscal year 2002 and the 3-year Rolling Plan in disarray; and so the judgment almost meant a 'cul-de-sac' for the federal government. Under Nigeria's vertical revenue sharing formula, federal, state and local governments are apportioned fixed percentage shares. Thus, the revenue in the Federation Account was shared as follows: federal government, 48.5 per cent; state government, 24 per cent; local government 20 per cent; and special funds, 7.5 per cent (see Table 1). Voiding of the first-line charge by the Supreme Court meant that the federal government can no longer appropriate additional revenue from the Federation Account. Accordingly, the federal government is not likely to have excess revenue and its mushrooming bureaucracy will diminish henceforth. Correspondingly, the influence of the federal government across the states would decline. Apparently, the Supreme Court's judgment favoured a more decentralized fiscal system and greater transparency and accountability in respect of federal finances.

The Universal Basic Education (UBE) programme of the PDP-controlled federal government remained one of the major casualties of the Supreme Court's judgment. Prior to the judgment, a new revenue bill was sent to the National Assembly for discussion and approval. For the importance attached to the UBE programme, a weight of 7.0 per cent was assigned to it in the proposed revenue allocation formula. It is shown in Table 3.1 that the federal government's relative share fell from 48.5 per cent to 41.5 per cent, while the proposed share of the state government was raised to 31.0 per cent so as to resolve the revenue-expenditure divergence. Primary education (the focus of the UBE programme) is the responsibility of the state governments. Therefore, the federal government could not appropriate the revenue allocated for this purpose. This put the effective delivery of the UBE in jeopardy. The judgment of the Supreme Court made the proposed revenue allocation formula unfavourable to the federal government and President Obasanjo subsequently withdrew the bill.

Consequent upon the ruling of the Supreme Court, the littoral state could no longer lay claim to the derivation revenue from crude oil from Nigeria's territorial waters, continental shelf and exclusive economic zone. A littoral state that produces oil, but from offshore, would lose revenue as a result. Crude oil production from Akwa Ibom State is mainly from offshore. The states recorded a quantum leap in its statutory revenue allocation from the Federation Account, rising from N6.0 billion in 2000 to N26.7 billion in 2001. The resultant fiscal crisis of the onshore/offshore oil dichotomy would stall development programmes for this state.

**Table 3.1: Vertical Revenue Allocation Scheme in Nigeria (Percentage Share)**

| Level of Government | Current Formula | Proposed Formula |
|---|---|---|
| 1. Federal Government | 48.5 | 41.5 |
| 2. State Governments | 24.0 | 31.0 |
| 3. Local Governments | 20.0 | 16.0 |
| 4. Special Funds | 7.5 | 3.6 |
| 5. Universal Basic Education (UBE) | - | 7.0 |
| 6. Federal Capital Territory | - | 1.0 |
| Total | 100.0 | 100.0 |

Source: Revenue Mobilization, Allocation and Fiscal Commission(RMAFC), Abuja.

Although Abia, Edo and Imo are oil-producing states, they are not bounded by sea. Therefore, they were not adversely affected by the ruling of the Supreme Court on littoral states and natural resources. For the following states – Rivers,

Delta, Ondo and Bayelsa – the revenue allocation to each of them on the basis of offshore crude oil is not negligible. They have lost revenue. However, these states would thenceforth get additional revenue from the application of the derivation principle to natural gas. The net effect on total revenue of the resource control suit on Bayelsa, Delta, Ondo and Rivers states is difficult to ascertain because data are hard to find. Non-oil-producing states are favoured by the Supreme Court judgment. A sizeable proportion of the crude oil produced in Nigeria is from offshore. The revenue from this source will be paid into the Federation Account and shared without the application of derivation and each state is expected to get an increased revenue allocation. This is why non-oil-producing, mostly northern states, may have celebrated the verdict.

Soon after the judgment, there were state-organized protests in the Niger Delta, indicative of the general despondency and dissatisfaction with the ruling of the Supreme Court on resource control. Feelings changed as top government officials made both young and old, together with various interest groups, aware of the unpleasant implications of the Supreme Court's resource control judgment. Indeed, impress accounts in government offices were put on hold in Akwa Ibom State. Hence, it should not be surprising that protests and demonstrations (see *Guardian* April 29, 2002, pp.17) against the Supreme Court's ruling were spearheaded by the state governors of the south-south (led by governor Attah of Akwa Ibom State) in order to enhance their chances of re-election into office. It should be recalled that the Supreme Court delivered its judgment at a time when clandestine moves and subterranean campaigns for the second term bid of the elected officials were in top gear. There was little doubt that strict adherence to the legal interpretation of the Supreme Court's judgment would have unequivocally had grave implications for the ruling party, PDP, in the 2003 general election.

Largely influenced by the premeditated negative reactions to the judgments by the people of the Niger Delta region, the federal government decided to set up a small committee headed by the Minister of Justice, Mr. Kanu Agabi who hails from Cross River, one of the oil-producing states, to examine the implications of the ruling. Following the total rejection of the onshore/offshore verdict and the recommendations of the Agabi committee, the federal government sought a political solution. A six-man committee with the Works and Housing Minister, Chief Tony Anenih, a powerful leader in the south-south zone and a close ally of President Obasanjo as head was appointed to build a political consensus on the issue. Consultations were still being conducted by the Anenih committee when the federal lawmakers muted the idea to impeach President Obasanjo. The onshore/offshore oil dichotomy was one of the seventeen impeachable offences listed by the legislators against Obasanjo. There were attempts to sponsor the onshore/offshore dichotomy abrogation bill by federal lawmakers from the south-south zone. It appeared that the federal lawmakers generally supported the abrogation of the onshore/offshore dichotomy. All this, together with pressure from the oil-producing states, led President Obasanjo to sponsor a bill seeking the abolition of the onshore/offshore dichotomy. It was difficult for the federal legislators to reject the bill since it had been listed as one of the impeachable offences of President Obasanjo. Expectedly, the bill was passed with a sense of urgency. However, before the bill was passed, the federal legislators changed 'contiguous zone' to 'continental shelf'. President Obasanjo withheld his assent to the bill as a result. The reason for this was that the continental shelf is up to 200 nautical miles as opposed to the contiguous zone that is within 24 nautical miles. The presidency rationalized its objection to the use of the continental shelf by the possibility of it leading to conflict between Nigeria and her neighbours. Currently, the bulk (about 40 per cent) of the oil production is within the contiguous zone.

Northern leaders were generally opposed to the substitution of 'continental shelf' for 'contiguous zone'. They advised the federal legislators not to override Mr. Obasanjo's veto of the bill because for them, it threatened the corporate existence of Nigeria. They argued that the use of 'continental shelf' tended to extend the territorial boundaries of the oil-producing states without going through the proper constitutional procedures. They also added that passing the bill into law would be inimical to the economies of non-oil states. As a result, northern elders urged northern legislators not to support any move to pass the bill in the interest of security, peace and stability.

Politicians and leading thinkers from the oil-producing region were generally happy about the Abrogation Bill. However the people of the Niger Delta have always doubted President Obasanjo on the sharing of oil wealth in Nigeria. It is generally acknowledged that it was during the period that Obasanjo was military Head of State (1976-1979) that the derivation principle was eliminated. Students of Nigeria's federal finance are aware that the report of the Aboyade Technical Committee on Revenue Allocation in 1977 did not favour the derivation principle. However, the federal military government rejected the recommendations of the Aboyade Technical Committee because they were too technical and incompatible with Nigeria's level of development. Reference was also made to Obasanjo's veto of the NDDC bill for which the National Assembly overrode his objections. For the Obasanjo administration to have allowed the judgment on the resource control suit at the time that the South-South zone had no judge in the Supreme Court (since the judgment came after the retirement of Adolphus Karibi-White JSC, from the South-South) is suggestive of Obasanjo's equivocal stand on derivation and resource control. Of course, the agreement of Obasanjo's position on oil dichotomy and that of the north's is a clear pointer to the regional struggle over the distribution of oil revenue. President Obasanjo's veto of the bill validated the fears of politicians and leaders of the South-South geo-political zone.

## Macro-economic Policy Implications of the Supreme Court Judgment

The likely effects of the Supreme Court (SC) judgment on the conduct of macro-economic policy are easily appreciated. Overall, the increase in the Federation

Account revenue implies that state and local governments will have more revenue to carry out their constitutionally assigned functions. In this sense, the vertical revenue-expenditure assignment imbalance is partly addressed and could ease inter-governmental fiscal conflict.

Arguably, the items on the first line charge which the SC voided in its judgment on April 5, 2002 served as fiscal handles. During the military regimes of Babangida (1985-93) and Abacha (1993-98), budgetary allocations to first line charge were arbitrarily determined. However, it is clear that when there was an increase in oil revenue more revenue was allocated to the first line charge and vice versa. To the extent that the federal government manipulated the revenue allocated to items on first line charge, it had some control over expenditures of state and local governments, which correlate highly with statutory revenue allocation from the Federation Account. Needless to say such fiscal handles, as applied to the Federation Account, will not be available henceforth. Thus, an important indirect control of expenditure of lower layers of government is dispensed with.

Effective conduct of macro-economic management under fiscal federalism rests mainly on the degree of expenditure centralization. Expenditure is highly centralized in Nigeria. Reported in Table 3.2 are actual total expenditure data for the period 1996 to 2000. Statistics show that the mean annual expenditure of the federal government accounted for more than 80 per cent of the total national expenditure in 1996-99, before declining to 60 per cent in 2000. Of course, if the federal government emphasizes the importance of sound macro-economic ma-nagement, it could exercise some control over total expenditure and, therefore, fiscal policy. Undoubtedly, state and local governments will be allocated more revenue from the Federation Account and the federal government less because of the SC judgment. As a result, assuming neutrality of other developments, the relative importance of state-local level expenditure will expectedly grow larger, thereby constraining effective conduct of fiscal policy. Indeed, relying on past fiscal behaviour, it is unlikely that expenditure of state and local governments will be in consonance with overall macro-economic policy objectives of the federal government.

### Table 3.2: Total Expenditure of Various Governments in Nigeria, 1996-2000

| Year | Federal (₦ billion) | % Share | State (₦ billion) | % Share | Local (₦ billion) | % Share | Total |
|------|-----|---------|-----|---------|-----|---------|-------|
| 1996 | 337.2 | 86.7 | 29.2 | 7.5 | 22.7 | 5.8 | 389.1 |
| 1997 | 428.2 | 87.0 | 33.4 | 6.8 | 31.3 | 6.2 | 492.2 |
| 1998 | 487.1 | 72.3 | 138.8 | 20.6 | 47.8 | 7.1 | 673.7 |
| 1999 | 947.7 | 80.9 | 163.1 | 13.9 | 60.4 | 5.2 | 1171.2 |
| 2000 | 701.1 | 59.7 | 342.2 | 29.2 | 131.2 | 11.1 | 1175.2 |

Source: Computed from Central Bank of Nigeria's *Annual Report and Statement of Account*, various issues.

There is a variant of this argument. The judgment of the Supreme Court favours a more decentralized fiscal arrangement. To a very large extent, state and local governments are statutorily independent in terms of their expenditure responsibilities. With the inevitable increase in the revenue of these levels of government, it may be difficult for the federal government to co-ordinate their spending activities and bring them in line with national macro-economic stability.

## Conclusion

This chapter has briefly examined the recent regional struggle for resource control in Nigeria. What emerges is the reinforcement of the ever-growing debate over regional competition for resources in the country. It is clear that the demand for a larger share of oil revenue by oil producing states was rejected because it meant the reduced comparative share of the dominant ethnic groups that control political power. At the National Political Reform Conference constituted by President Obasanjo in 2005, the insistence of the delegates from the south-south zone that derivation principle should be given a larger weight of not less than 25 per cent brought the conference to an awkward end. This undoubtedly underpins the unremitting nature of regional competition for resources in Nigeria.

## References

Adebayo, A. G., 1990, 'The "Ibadan School" and the Handling of Federal Finance in Nigeria', *The Journal of Modern African Studies*, Vol. 28, No. 2, pp. 245-264.

Ayodele, O. S., Egwaikhide, F. O., Isumonah, V. A. and Oyeranti, O. A., 2005, 'Supreme Court Judgement and Aftermaths', in Akinola A. Owosekun, Ode Ojowu & Festus O. Egwaikhide, eds., *Contemporary Issues in the Management of the Nigerian Economy*, Ibadan: NISER, pp. 361-382.

Awobajo, S. A., 1981, 'An Analysis of Oil Spill in Nigeria, 1976-1980', paper presented at the seminar on the Petroleum Industry and Nigerian Environment, organized by the Nigeria National Petroleum Corporation (NNPC) at the Petroleum Training Institute (PTI), Warri, 9-12 December.

Chick, A. L., 1953, *Report of the Fiscal Commissioner on Financial Effects of Proposed New Constitutional Arrangements*, Lagos: Government Printer.

Due, J. F. and Friedlaender, A. F., 1977, *Government Finance: Economics of the Public Sector*, Illinois: D. Richard.

Egwaikhide, F. O. and Aregbeyen, O., 1999, 'Oil Production Externalities in the Niger Delta: Is Fiscal Solution Feasible?', *Proceedings of the 1999 Annual Conference of the Nigerian Economic Society*, pp. 101-115.

Emenuga, C., 1993, 'Nigeria: The Search for an Acceptable Revenue Allocation Formula', *Proceedings of the 1993 Annual Conference of the Nigerian Economic Society*, pp. 79-105.

Hicks, J. R. and Phillipson, S., 1951, *Report of the Commission on Revenue Allocation*, Lagos: Government Printer.

Hutchful, E., 1970, 'Oil Companies and Environmental Pollution in Nigeria', in Ake, C. ed., *Political Economy of Nigeria*, London: Longman, pp. 113-141.

Mbanefoh, G. F., 1986, 'Military Presence and the Future of Nigerian Fiscal Federalism', *Faculty of the Social Sciences Lecture Series*, No.1, University of Ibadan.

Mbanefoh, G. F., 1993, 'Unsettled Issues in Nigerian Fiscal Federalism and the National Question', *Proceedings of the 1993 Annual Conference of the Nigerian Economic Society*, pp. 61-77.

Mbanefoh, G. F and Egwaikhide, F. O., 1998, 'Revenue Allocation in Nigeria: Derivation Principle Revisited', in Amuwo, K., A. A. Agbaje, R. T. Suberu and G. Herault eds., *Federalism and Political Restructuring in Nigeria*, Ibadan: Spetrum Books and Institute Francais de Recherche en Afrique (IFRA), Chap. 14.

Musgrave, R. A. and P. B. Musgrave, 1980, *Public Finance in Theory and Practice*, London: McGraw-Hill.

Norregaard, J., 1995, 'Intergovernmental Fiscal Relations', in Shome, P., ed., *Tax Policy Handbook*, Washington DC: International Monetary Fund, pp. 247-253.

Okigbo, P., 1980, *Report of the Revenue Allocation Commission*, Lagos: Government Printer.

Phillips, A. O., 1971, 'Nigeria's Federal Financial Experience', *Journal of Modern African Studies*, Vol. 9, pp. 389-408.

Phillips, A. O. (1975) 'Revenue Allocation in Nigeria, 1970-1980', *The Nigerian Journal of Economics and Social Studies*, Vol. 17, No. 3, pp. 1-28.

Phillipson, S., 1948, *Administrative and Financial Procedure under the New Constitution: Financial Relations Between the Government of Nigeria and the Native Administration*, Lagos: Government Printer.

Raiseman, J. and Tress, R. C., 1958, *Preliminary Report of the Fiscal Commission*, Lagos: Government Printer.

Stewart, F. and Ghani, E., 1991, 'How Significant are Externalities for Development?', *World Development*, Vol. 19, pp. 569-594.

Teriba, O., 1966, 'Nigerian Revenue Allocation Experience', *Nigerian Journal of Economics and Social Studies*, Vol. 8, No. 3, pp. 361-382.

# 4

---

# Educational Facilities and their Beneficiaries

## Introduction

In this chapter, the zonal distribution of educational establishments is used to give detail on the associated benefits of a federal presence or lack of it. However, the analysis focuses on federal universities due to the availability of data and, more importantly, the perception of a university education from the beginning as being not just an instrument of manpower development but also of the (re)distribution of resources. As Young (1981:146) wrote about the idea of university in Africa,

> Universities also...above all...became gatekeepers of social mobility. In most African states, a university diploma bestowed not only intellectual grace but also access to most of the higher-salaried and prestige-conveying positions in society. Its faculty enjoyed a very high status, especially in the early years of independence. Thus, universities from the onset were not only repositories of universalistic values, but also arenas of competition for scarce societal resources.

The data used are mainly National Universities Commission (NUC) published student enrolment figures, capital and recurrent allocations to the universities by the federal government. These are available only up to the 1991-92 session. It is therefore not the choice of the authors to stop at that particular year. The 1987-88 session was lost due to cumulative sundry disturbances from which most federal universities are yet to regain a normal academic year of September/October-June/July.[1]

The conclusions about beneficiaries and losers are based on a few assumptions. One is the assumption of a uniform cost of providing university education to all students. In reality, the cost per student varies with the course of study. Science courses are more costly to run than arts courses as can be seen from Table 4.1 Medicine is the costliest of all courses. This means that zones that have more students doing costlier courses in their share of total student enrolment are greater beneficiaries of federal expenditure on education. A related assumption is that all enrolled students successfully completed their programme whereas some students in reality dropped out some time before their successful colleagues completed their programme. The conclusions do not take misappropriation into account, which is believed to be rampant in the university.

### Table 4.1: Unit Cost (₦) per Student for Science-based and Arts-based Courses, Academic Sessions 1985/86 and 1986/87

| University | Sciences | Arts |
|---|---|---|
| Lagos | 1,720.06 | 949.45 |
| Nsukka | 1,770.42 | 865.89 |
| Jos | 2,306.39 | 714.50 |
| Calabar | 2,288.61 | 873.46 |
| Owerri | 1,609.76 | 2,231.88 |
| Minna | 2,459.29 | Nil |

Source: NUC Approved Revised Parameters for Allocation of Recurrent Grants of Federally Funded Universities, May 1990.

In the same vein, the geo-ethnic origins of the academic members of staff of the federal universities are not taken into account in the measurement of the regional distribution of benefit from resources expended on universities because 'higher education, and the university in particular, depends on academic excellence of accepted international standards for its survival' (Briggs 1980:72). As Briggs (1980:73) further observes, the impact of the federal government on the geo-ethnic distribution of academic staff, that is, federal presence, can at best be measured by 'selection for and funding of post-graduate and staff development programmes'. Yet, he argues that 'the most crucial aspect ... is... the provision of higher educational facilities, that is, the external economies of establishing and operating higher educational institutions' (p. 73). Thus, it suffices to dwell on the geo-ethnic distribution of federal schools and the ethno-distribution of the benefit of the cost of running them.

Of course, the universities receive all kinds of grants and allocations from the government. These are research grants, teaching and equipment grants, allocations for capital projects, special capital grants for the rehabilitation of existing facilities, library development grants, etc. The irregular manner of disbursement and uses make the data which some of them present quite difficult to employ for measuring the regional distribution of the benefit of federal government's investment in education. Some of the grants are not fully allocated within the year and have to be carried over haphazardly while in some cases allocated grants are diverted to other uses.

Allocations for research not completed or satisfactorily completed, for example, have often led to the withholding of allocations in subsequent years from a university by NUC. Sometimes, NUC allows the university to carry over unutilized research grants. There are differentials in the total number and overall quality of staff as a determinant of the size of allocation that a university gets, especially for research grants. This is observed from the pattern in which older universities – Ibadan,

Nsukka, Zaria, Lagos, Ile-Ife and Benin - tend to receive higher amounts than the rest (see Table 4.2).

## Table 4.2: Research Grant Allocations, 1987-1992 (₦)

| University | 1987 | 1988 | 1989 | 1990 | 1991 | 1992 |
|---|---|---|---|---|---|---|
| Ibadan | 1,379,000 | 2,152,000 | 2,088,414 | 2,561,341 | 2,440,163 | 2,158,349 |
| Lagos | 1,264,000 | 1,972,500 | 1,911,311 | 2,347,812 | 2,256,000 | 1,480,011 |
| Nsukka | 1,276,000 | 1,991,500 | 1,955,598 | 2,398,449 | 2,562,938 | 1,853,611 |
| Zaria | 1,447,000 | 2,257,000 | 2,159,656 | 2,648,716 | 1,757,224 | 1,403,834 |
| Ile-Ife | 1,245,000 | 1,943,500 | 1,879,908 | 2,305,618 | 2,516,898 | 1,494,521 |
| Benin | 900,000 | 1,428,500 | 1,379,479 | 1,691,866 | 2,133,224 | 975,792 |
| Jos | 655,000 | 1,024,500 | 1,012,747 | 1,242,086 | 1,339,020 | 584,025 |
| Calabar | 587,000 | 917,500 | 918,459 | 1,126,447 | 943,837 | 627,534 |
| Kano | 526,000 | 823,500 | 820,355 | 1,006,126 | 679,102 | 399,023 |
| Maiduguri | 637,000 | 995,500 | 987,262 | 1,210,831 | 1,058,938 | 540,495 |
| Sokoto | 391,000 | 612,500 | 625,501 | 767,147 | 571,673 | 170,492 |
| Ilorin | 599,000 | 936,500 | 931,808 | 1,142,819 | 1,431,102 | 674,711 |
| Port Harcourt | 473,000 | 741,500 | 831,732 | 926,916 | 1,277,633 | 623,927 |
| Owerri | 206,000 | 324,500 | 358,665 | 439,885 | 533,306 | 217,650 |
| Akure | 131,000 | 208,500 | 250,107 | 306,745 | 387,510 | 159,610 |
| Bauchi | 187,000 | 295,500 | 328,103 | 402,403 | 471,918 | 126,964 |
| Minna | 120,000 | 191,500 | 231,971 | 284,500 | 310,775 | 170,492 |
| Yola | 113,000 | 179,500 | 221,179 | 271,265 | 234,041 | 119,708 |
| Makurdi | 193,000 | 304,500 | 337,796 | 414,291 | - | - |
| Abeokuta | 184,000 | 171,500 | 213,456 | 261,794 | - | - |
| Total | 12,513,000 | 19,472,000 | 19,443,507 | 23,757,057 | 22,905,302 | 13,923,000 |

Source: NUC Research Bulletin, December 1993.

The measurement of federal presence in the educational sector in this chapter will, therefore, be limited to recurrent and capital expenditures. There is no denying the fact that capital expenditure has substantial multiplier effects on the local economy. However, capital allocations are presented here merely as a graphic illustration because they are not as easily amenable to statistical analysis and deductions as student enrolments (see Table 4.3). By the nature of their use, namely, investment in fixed or durable assets, capital allocations do not carry a once-and-for-all cost per head implication. That means that they are not as equally useful as recurrent expenditure for the calculation of benefit or disadvantage on a regional basis. Yet, capital allocations presented in Table 2 indicate the following descending order of beneficiaries: South-West, South-South, North-West, North-Central, South-East and North-East. The South received ₦2,820 million against the North's ₦2,272.4 million during the period (1987-1992).

Table 4.3: Capital Allocation to Universities (1976/77-1998) in ₦

| University | Zone 1 | Zone 2 | Zone 3 | Zone 4 | Zone 5 | Zone 6 | Total |
|---|---|---|---|---|---|---|---|
| Ibadan | 345,269,683 | | | | | | 345,269,683 |
| Lagos | 280,566,845 | | | | | | 280,566,845 |
| Nsukka | | 375,584,876 | | | | | 375,584,876 |
| Zaria | | | 361,531,321 | | | | 361,531,321 |
| Ile-Ife | 304,016,987 | | | | | | 304,016,987 |
| Benin | | | | | | 312,495,404 | 312,495,404 |
| Jos | | | | | 224,494,267 | | 224,494,267 |
| Calabar | | | | | | 246,694,017 | 246,694,017 |
| Kano | | | 217,606,008 | | | | 217,606,008 |
| Maiduguri | | | | 221,267,287 | | | 221,267,287 |
| Sokoto | | | 255,806,865 | | | | 255,806,865 |
| Ilorin | | | | | 234,076,351 | | 234,076,351 |
| Port Harcourt | | | | | | 243,853,219 | 243,853,219 |
| Owerri | | 198,509,854 | | | | | 198,509,854 |
| Akure | 173,241,004 | | | | | | 173,241,004 |
| Bauchi | | | | 194,318,954 | | | 194,318,954 |
| Minna | | | | | 171,618,514 | | 171,618,514 |
| Yola | | | | 171,921,035 | | | 171,921,035 |
| Makurdi | | | | | 85,038,584 | | 85,038,584 |
| Abeokuta | 60,151,452 | | | | | | 60,151,452 |
| Abuja | | | | | 132,764,879 | | 132,764,879 |
| Uyo | | | | | | 138,031,788 | 138,031,788 |
| Awka | | 141,466,317 | | | | | 141,466,317 |
| Total | 1,163,245,971 | 715,561,047 | 834,944,194 | 587,507,276 | 847,992,595 | 941,073,429 | 5,092,325,515 |

Computed from Source: *National Universities Commission Statistical Digest*, various issues.

## The Development of Education in Nigeria

The provision of modern/formal or western education in Nigeria began in the Benin Empire in 1515 with the efforts of Portuguese merchants and much later in Abeokuta in 1843 and other southern Nigerian towns such as Onitisha in 1858 with the efforts of Christian missionaries (Fafunwa 1991). Gradually, schools sprang up in many parts of southern Nigeria. Initially, the British colonial government participated in the development of education indirectly by distributing grants to missionaries in support of their educational efforts. Later, it began establishing and enforcing standards through the inspectorate system and procedures for giving grants and scholarships as well as establishing schools with financial contributions from communities, all in the south-west before the beginning of the twentieth century. At the same time, individuals and commercial firms established and managed schools. 'By the end of 1912 there were fifty-nine government primary schools and ninety-one mission schools aided by the government' (Fafunwa 1991: 97). The colonial government established the first secondary school, King's College, in Lagos in 1909.

The first government elementary primary school in the north was founded in Kano in 1909. Thus, the northern part of Nigeria was virtually left 'out of the match' of western education. As indicated above, Christian missionaries whose evangelization was intertwined with the founding of schools, account for the southern part's huge edge over the northern part in educational development. This has often been explained in terms of the then tendency of Islam, the latter's dominant religion, to be averse to the penetration of Christian missionary activities. As the argument goes, Islam slowed down the progress of western education in the north. Its logic is simple. Had the spread of western education followed an unreligious path, the north would have embraced it, with the initial gap between it and the south in the distribution of educational facilities and subscription to western education kept to a minimum. Fafunwa (1991) rejects this and argues instead that missionary-driven education did not only slow down the progress of western education in the north but that it also did in the south-west where Islam and Christian religions have a roughly equal number of faithful. This suggests that the explanation for the difference between the northern and southern parts of Nigeria in education must be sought elsewhere.

On a general note, the role of the British colonial government in educational development throughout Nigeria was despicable in the opinion even of non-Nigerian observers as by 1992 there were only 195 Government and Assisted schools, and 2,432 Unassisted schools in Nigeria. In 1920 the Phelps-Stokes Fund, an American philanthropic organization, and the International Education Board were alarmed by this situation and set up two commissions on education in Africa. The report on West, South and Equatorial Africa was released in 1922 and that on East, Central and South Africa in 1924. They criticized the 'lackadaisical' attitude of the British colonial government's attitude to the development of education in Africa. In response and as evidence of a change in attitude, the government proceeded to issue a policy on education whose essential thrusts were the tightening up of standards and the joining of forces with the people for the expansion of education.

Thus, the colonial government made educational expansion dependent on the participation of the people. It follows that the intrinsic value each person attached to education, not external propping, would count greatly in their proportional share of the total number of educational establishments and school enrolment. This fact and the retarding influence of Christian evangelization for even a short time on educational expansion in the Yoruba, western Nigeria, reported by Fafunwa (1991), indicates that Christian missionary activities can neither take the sole credit nor blame for educational development anywhere in Nigeria. Fafunwa (1991:131) reports:

> Education in the Yoruba country suffered a severe temporary set-back in 1931 as a result of a 'revivalist' movement under the leadership of one Joseph Babalola. Although the first effect of this emotional mass movement was to fill schools and

churches, later it became antagonistic to such temporal superfluities as secular education and almost emptied the schools, reducing the attendance at many by as much as 90 per cent; it was not until the following year that recovery took place.

Hence achievements in 'Nigeriansation' and the self-government of nationalist struggles unevenly spurred the demand for more educational facilities.

While the pioneering and zealous role of Christian missionaries in the expansion of educational opportunities is beyond question, parents, communities and relatives' equally catalytic or non-catalytic role deserves acknowledgement. In the southern part of Nigeria, massive self-help efforts came from 'parents, clubs, organizations, and ethnic groups' into the expansion of educational facilities (Fafunwa 1991:140). Begun by the Yoruba with particular reference to higher education overseas, this self-help effort took on competition between ethnic groups when the Ibibio and Igbo joined the Yoruba in the 1930s in sponsoring their protégés to acquire university education abroad.

Yet, government intervention bestowed some startup advantages on certain parts of Nigeria and its communities. In 1929, the colonial government centralized education with its assumption of greater responsibility in standard setting and the involvement in, and direction of, expansion. This culminated in several reforms at various intervals. For example, in 1930, E. Hussey, Director of Education, proposed a 3-stage education of six years in primary school in the first stage, six years in intermediate school in the second stage and a third stage at a higher level; this led to the establishment of Yaba Higher College in 1932. The western part of Nigeria was thus blessed with the advantage of being the host of the first higher institution of learning in Nigeria even though the college soon suffered terribly, to the point of being moribund, from the effects of the Second World War. The West again clinched another advantage from the increasing interest of the colonial government in educational expansion in Nigeria when University College, Ibadan, was founded in 1948 following the report of the Elliot Commission on which, for the first time, three African educators served (Fafunwa 1991).

On the eve of political independence, the federal government set up what is now known as the Ashby Commission to help ascertain Nigeria's needs in postsecondary education in twenty years from that time. With Professor K.O. Dike, Sir Kashim Ibrahim and Dr. Sanya Onabamiro representing the tripod regional character of that time on the commission, regional interests were bound to take a prime consideration of one or two members' input into its report. It is this feeling that underlies the argument of Yoloye (1989) that 'federal character principle', that became a directive principle in the Nigerian constitution in 1979 and is in the subsisting 1999 constitution, has its origins in the acceptance of the minority report of Dr. Onabamiro, Western Region's Minister of Education. The minority report rejected the majority report that could have put paid to the plan of the Western Region to start its own university. Consequently, three universities came into existence at Zaria, Nsukka and Ile-Ife. In 1977, the federal government under General Olusegun Obasanjo from the south-west, created seven new universities 'to correct an apparent imbalance in the geographical spread of these institutions' (Oladapo 1987:61).

In a subtle reference to the distribution of government-owned educational institutions, Section 18 enjoins the operators of the 1999 constitution as in the 1979 constitution to ensure the provision of equal educational opportunities for all wherever they are in Nigeria. The underlying philosophy is perhaps fair-play in the sharing of common resources and the location of national institutions (Briggs 1980). This is why the federal government endeavours to establish new schools in places where it realizes that there are no federal schools.

## Educational Facilities and Federal Presence

The view of higher education as a 'public good' in Nigeria was for a long time derived from its conception as an instrument for the creation of human capital in the development process (Kwanashie 1987). Public opinion linked university education to development from the beginning even though this was unstated, for example, in the Fourth National Development Plan. With regards to a federal presence, education is an issue because it is not just a private but also a public good. It is specifically so from the multiplier effects of the geo-ethnic share of student enrolment and location of the educational institution. The multiplier effect of the location of an educational establishment is evident in the share of student enrolment by the state in which the federal university is located (see tables 7-16). It is also felt by the geo-ethnic group that is predominant in that location and its environs in the area of employment and the local economy. There is no gainsaying then that simply the presence of an educational institution, particularly the tertiary type, boosts the local economy as evident in housing and transportation.

The federal government has participated in the provision of all levels of educational facilities – primary, secondary, intermediate and university (see tables 4-7). It founded some and took over others for different reasons. It took over regional/state universities at Ile-Ife and Zaria in 1977 to express its decision to be in sole charge of university education in Nigeria. The universities at Nsukka and Benin had been voluntarily handed over to the federal government by their owner states or regions in 1971 and 1975 respectively for financial incapability (NUC Secretariat 1987). Between 1977 and 1980, all universities were federally owned unlike in the United States of America where the federal government owns only one university (cited in Oladapo 1987). In 1977 the issue of federal presence became even more serious because federal universities stopped charging tuition fees while what they could charge on lodging and board was pegged by federal government. Hence, the federal government took over some universities, polytechnics and secondary schools not for the reason it took over Ife and Zaria but in order to immediately register federal presence in the provision of an educational facility in the affected states.

## Table 4.4: Distribution of Federal Government/Science/Technical Colleges

| Zone | Number per State | Zonal Total |
|------|------------------|-------------|
| 1 | Ekiti (4), Lagos (4), Ogun (3), Ondo (3), Osun (3), Oyo (2) | 19 |
| 2 | Abia (3), Anambra (3), Ebonyi (2), Enugu (2), Imo (2) | 12 |
| 3 | Jigawa (2), Kaduna (3), Kano (2), Katsina (2), Kebbi (3), Sokoto (3), Zamfara (2) | 17 |
| 4 | Adamawa (3), Bauchi (2), Borno (3), Gombe (2), Taraba (3), Yobe (2) | 15 |
| 5 | Benue (4), Kogi (2), Kwara (2), Nassarawa (2), Niger (5), Plateau (2), FCT (6) | 23 |
| 6 | Akwa Ibom (3), Bayelsa (3), Cross River (3), Delta (2), Edo (3), Rivers (3) | 17 |
| Total | | 103 |

Source: Federal Ministry of Education, Abuja 2001-2004 Admission Returns and Requests.

## Table 4.5: Distribution of Federal Colleges of Education

| Zone | Number per State | Zonal Total |
|------|------------------|-------------|
| 1 | Ekiti (0), Lagos (1), Ogun (1), Ondo (1), Osun (0), Oyo (1) | 4 |
| 2 | Abia (0), Anambra (1), Ebonyi (0), Enugu (1), Imo (0) | 2 |
| 3 | Jigawa (0), Kaduna (1), Kano (2), Katsina (1), Kebbi (0), Sokoto (1), Zamfara (0) | 5 |
| 4 | Adamawa (1), Bauchi (1), Borno (0), Gombe (0), Taraba (0), Yobe (1) | 3 |
| 5 | Benue, Kogi (1), Kwara, Nassarawa, Niger (1), Plateau (1), FCT(0) | 3 |
| 6 | Akwa Ibom (0), Bayelsa (0), Cross River (1), Delta (1), Edo (0), Rivers (1) | 3 |
| Total | | 20 |

Source: Federal Ministry of Education, Colleges of Education Department, 2004.

## Table 4.6: Distribution of Federal Polytechnics

| Zone | Number per State | Zonal Total |
|------|------------------|-------------|
| 1 | Ekiti (1), Lagos (1), Ogun (1), Ondo (0), Osun (1), Oyo (0) | 4 |
| 2 | Abia (0), Anambra (1), Ebonyi (1), Enugu (0), Imo (1) | 3 |
| 3 | Jigawa (0), Kaduna (1), Kano (0), Katsina (0), Kebbi (0), Sokoto (1), Zamfara (0) | 2 |
| 4 | Adamawa (1), Bauchi (1), Borno (0), Gombe (0), Taraba (0), Yobe (0) | 2 |
| 5 | Benue (0), Kogi (1), Kwara (1), Nassarawa (1), Niger (1), Plateau (0), FCT (0) | 4 |
| 6 | Akwa Ibom (0), Bayelsa (0), Cross River (0), Delta (0), Edo (1), Rivers (0) | 1 |
| Total | | 16 |

Source: Federal Ministry of Education, Polytechnics Department, 2004.

### Table 4.7: Distribution of Federal Universities*

| Zone | Number per State | Zonal Total |
|---|---|---|
| 1 | Ekiti (0), Lagos (1), Ogun (1), Ondo (1), Osun (1), Oyo (1) | 5 |
| 2 | Abia (1), Anambra (1), Ebonyi (0), Enugu (1), Imo (1) | 4 |
| 3 | Jigawa (0), Kaduna (2), Kano (1), Katsina (0), Kebbi (0), Sokoto (1), Zamfara (0) | 4 |
| 4 | Adamawa (1), Bauchi (1), Borno (1), Gombe (0), Taraba (0), Yobe (0) | 3 |
| 5 | Benue (1), Kogi (0), Kwara (1), Nassarawa (0), Niger (1), Plateau (1), FCT (1) | 5 |
| 6 | Akwa Ibom (1), Bayelsa (0), Cross River (1), Delta (0), Edo (1), Rivers (1) | 3 |
| Total | | 24 |

Source: NUC Statistical Bulletin, 2004

* List excludes degree-awarding federal colleges of education, which are counted among federal-owned colleges of education.
Notes: Index of Composition of Zones

| Zone | Constituent States |
|---|---|
| 1 | Ekiti, Lagos, Ogun, Ondo, Osun, Oyo (South-West) |
| 2 | Abia, Anambra, Ebonyi, Enugu, Imo (South-East) |
| 3 | Jigawa, Kaduna, Kano, Katsina, Kebbi. Sokoto, Zamfara (North-West) |
| 4 | Adamawa, Bauchi, Borno, Gombe, Taraba, Yobe (North-East) |
| 5 | Benue, Kogi, Kwara, Nassarawa, Niger, Plateau, FCT (North-Central) |
| 6 | Akwa Ibom, Bayelsa, Cross River, Delta, Edo, Rivers (South-South) |

From Tables 4.4-4.7, the South-West leads overall in the number of federal schools. The North-Central's share of federal secondary schools is boosted by that of the Federal Capital Territory (FCT), which has the ambiguous status of being part of that zone and a national territory to which all states or Nigerians can lay claim. If, indeed, FCT is a national territory that belongs to all Nigerians, the North-Central's share of federal secondary schools drops behind that of the South-West. The same applies to the distribution of universities. The other advantage of the South-West with regards to the location of universities is that it took exactly a half share (three out of six) of the first or oldest universities for a period of twenty-nine years, between 1948 and 1977. The South-South zone has the least share of federal polytechnics (see Table 4.6). However it fares comparably with other zones in the share of federal secondary schools. On the other hand, the South-East has the least share of federal secondary schools and colleges of education.

The disparities in the distribution of federal educational establishments have a close link with the disparities in each region's share of the total number of states at various times since the distribution is on the basis of states. The South-South and South-East zones' smaller shares in federal schools, as earlier noted, were the results of their being circumscribed in very few states for a long time.

The creation of a state immediately makes obvious the issue of federal presence in it. For example, the creation of Bayelsa State in 1996 made obvious the lack of federal presence there in terms of the national electric power grid, roads, educational establishments, etc as it was not part of the old Rivers State. The federal government has been compelled to act not only by the demand for federal presence that follows the laying bare of the lack of it but also out of its concern for the even distribution of educational facilities among the states that make up geopolitical zones. Consequently, geo-ethnic groups that have more states/polical administrative units are at an advantage to have more share of federal educational institutions. The age of the state factor in the distributional patterns of educational establishments in Nigeria among the states supports the view that the earlier a state is achieved by a conscious and influential geo-ethnic group, the more likely it is to have any given type of federal school. The distribution of federal universities among the states further illustrates this. All states created by 1987, except Katsina which may be explained in terms of absence of demand, has a federal university each.

However, the distribution of federal institutions can also be explained in terms of historical accident between the consideration of both the federal and state governments at different times of particular cities' status as administrative headquarters for the location of educational establishments. Hence, some states have a disproportionate number of some types of educational establishments compared to others within the same geopolitical zone. It is observed in Table 4, for example, that Kaduna State has two federal universities where Jigawa, Katsina, Kebbi and Zamfara states have none. This pattern began first with the establishment of a regional university at Zaria near the town of Kaduna, both in the present Kaduna State, by the government of the Northern Region in 1962. Later, the federal government established a military university at Kaduna most likely because of Kaduna, as a key administrative and urban centre, having the requisites for hosting such an institution. Therefore it could not be said that Kaduna State has two federal universities. The decision of the federal government to take over regional/ state-owned universities in 1977 and the pattern of states creation that followed changed the distribution equation. This explanation holds for old Oyo State in the South-West geopolitical zone before the creation of Osun State in 1991. Prior to this time, Oyo State had two universities in Ibadan and Ife whose catchment area covered Ondo, the present Ekiti; Lagos; and Ogun states in the South-West zone.

Being unmindful of existing distribution patterns, arbitrary and dominated by 'political leverage, sectional rivalry, control, and pre-emptive action', state reorganization has often altered the geo-political distribution of federal schools (Yoloye 1989: 48). Consequently, federal educational presence becomes an issue in some places unless the federal government is conscious of fulfilling its constitutional duty as regards 'federal character' in the distribution of its educational establishments.

### Instruments of Facilitation or Control

The concern with equitable or equal access to university education led to the strengthening of existing government institutions for co-ordinating the admission and other processes of federal universities. National Universities Commission (NUC) and the Joint Admissions and Matriculation Board (JAMB) mostly fit this observation, hence a comment on them is appropriate here.

The government of Alhaji Tafawa Balewa initially set up the NUC in 1962 on the recommendation of the Ashby Commission as an intermediary between government and the then two federal and three regional universities (Aminu 1987, Abdulkadir 1987, NUC 1987). As an administrative organ of government, the NUC was to perform an advisory function on funding and channelling of all funding to the universities. Its functions were expanded to include oversight when it was reconstituted into a statutory body by Decree No.1 of 1974 under an executive secretary from 1975.

## NUC

The geo-ethnic profiles of the NUC's executive secretaries from 1975, when it effectively became a statutory body, suggest inter-regional tension over the control of the development of university education. All executive secretaries appointed by heads of state of northern origin from 1975 to 1999 (a period of twenty-four years) were northerners. The only exception is Abel I. Guobadia from the South-South geopolitical zone who assumed the position from the office of Director of Planning in an acting capacity in 1979 when Dr. Jubril Aminu went on sabbatical leave. He served as such until 1981 when Alhaji Yahaya Aliyu was appointed executive secretary. Prof. Peter Okebukola from the South-West geopolitical zone was appointed executive secretary in 1999 by the incumbent head of state who is also from the South-West (see Table 8). He was succeeded by Professor Julius Okogie (South-South) in July 2006.

**Table 4.8: National Universities Commission Executive Secretaries, 1975 to Date**

| No. | Name | Post | Date |
|-----|------|------|------|
| 1. | Dr. Jibril Aminu | Executive Secretary | 1975-1979 |
| 2. | Dr. Abel I. Goubadia | Ag. Executive Secretary | 1979-1981 |
| 3. | Alhaji Yahaya Aliyu | Executive Secretary | 1981-1986 |
| 4. | Prof. Idris Abdulkadir | Executive Secretary | 1986-1996 |
| 5. | Prof. Munzali Jibril | Executive Secretary | 1996-1999 |
| 6. | Prof. Peter Okebukola | Executive Secretary | 1999 to June 2006 |
| 7. | Prof. Julius Okogie | Executive Secretary | June 2006 - |

Source: NUC Secretariat Statistical Information 1998.

## JAMB

The federal government under General Murtala Muhammed, a northerner, set up the National Commission on University Entrance in December 1975 to examine the problems of admission into universities. It proceeded to set up JAMB before the Committee could complete its assignment in April 1977 under General Olusegun Obasanjo from the South-West (Ike 1986). If the original motive behind the creation of JAMB was free of ethnic rivalry, its charge under President Shehu Shagari (North-West) to enforce a quota principle for admission into federal universities betrayed this. This ethno-regional undertone is evident from its untainted northern headship from inception to date (see Table 9). The northern headship of JAMB initiated by a southern head of state that has also retained it as renewed by his successive northern heads of state does not detract from this observation. The retention of this headship by a southern head of state should be understood as his balancing of the replacement of northern by southern headship of the NUC.

### Table 4.9: JAMB Registrars, 1977 to Date

| No. | Name | State/region | Date |
|-----|------|--------------|------|
| 1. | Mr. Michael Sunday Angulu | Niger state/North | 1977-1986 |
| 2. | Dr. M. Shaibawa Abdulralman | Niger state/North | 1986-1995 |
| 3. | Prof. Bello Ahmad Salim | Kano/North | 1995-2006 |
| 4. | Prof. Dibu Ojerinde | Oyo/South | 2006 to date |

Source: *JAMB Brochure*, various Issues, Abuja.

Prior to JAMB, the conduct of admission into the university was observed not to be cost-effective or efficient. Candidates had to pay multiple application fees. Some of these received admission from two or more universities and in the course of choosing from them, denied others admission. Yet, others tragically found themselves rejected after paying multiple application fees. Awareness of these problems led the Committee of Vice-Chancellors (CVC) in 1974 to set up a committee of foreign experts, namely, secretaries of admission councils from the United Kingdom and Province of Ontario, Canada, to review admission processes in Nigeria. However the CVC for unexplained reasons failed to act on its report to set up a common admissions body as the committee of vice-chancellors from the UK did in setting up the Universities Central Admissions Council. From its terms of reference to the panel, it seems the reason was their being jealous of their 'standards and traditions' (Angulu 1987:109). Thus the result was that the federal government imposed JAMB on universities in 1977 by which time it had taken over all of them.

In August 1981, the federal government under President Shehu Shagari issued 'Guidelines for Admissions [quota system] in Federal Universities', to be sure 'that admissions into Federal Universities reflected the Federal Character as enunciated in the constitution' (cited in Ike 1986:147). JAMB first applied these as follows in 1983 even though admission on the basis of quota was not the original idea behind it. These were merit (40 per cent), locality (30 per cent), educationally less developed (ELD) (20 per cent) and discretion (10 per cent) to be applied by the six oldest universities – Ibadan (South-West), Zaria (North-West), Benin (South-South), Ile-Ife (South-West), Lagos (South-West), Nsukka (South-East). The guidelines for the seven new universities at Calabar (South-South), Ilorin (North-Central), Jos

(North-Central), Maiduguri (North-East), Port Harcourt (South-South) and So-koto (North-West) were as follows: merit (30 per cent), locality (30 per cent), ELD (30 per cent) and discretion (10 per cent). The new universities of technology that the federal government created were to apply the guidelines in the order of merit (20 per cent) and discretion (80 per cent).

The federal government made an addition to the guidelines, which spelt out 'locality' of each university as 'catchment area' in 1983 with a scheme of inducement grants for compliance and penalty for non-compliance (Ike 1986). Locality varied per state and per university. Its definition with regards to a university may seem to have nothing in particular to do with its location. As Ike (1986:151) observes: 'A concept of "locality" which considers Plateau State part of the locality for the University of Ife, or Benue State part of the locality for the University of Calabar, or Rivers States (sic) part of the locality for the Federal University of Technology, Minna, beats the imagination of ordinary mortals.' However, on closer scrutiny, the location of a university does as such highlight the importance of the existence of a federal university in the location of a candidate's state of origin. This is illustrated by Oyo State's experience in the 1984/85 academic session. Angulu (1987:112-3) writes:

> Thus, in the 1984/85 session, Oyo State, which apart from its ability to subscribe candidates to all the universities by merit and had the universities of Ibadan, Ife and Ilorin to which it could subscribe under the locality criterion had the highest number of candidates admitted, 3,348 or 14.2 per cent of the total admissions, whereas in terms of the total number of applications, it came fourth to Imo, Bendal and Anambra which are comparably educationally developed.

The state government under Chief Bola Ige vicariously confirmed Oyo State's advantage by not joining his counterpart Unity Party of Nigeria (UPN) governments in Lagos, Ogun, Bendel and Ondo (all except Bendel in the South-West geopolitical zone), to establish a state university. These state governments; the then only two in the South-East zone (Anambra and Imo) and the remaining two in the South-South zone (Cross River and Rivers), had established their universities between 1981 and 1983 'to provide avenues for the large number of students leaving the secondary school system, who would find it increasingly difficult to get into federal universities because of the quota system' (Oladapo 1986:64).

Locality was defined deliberately to confer privilege on eleven states identified as educationally less developed, namely, Bauchi, Benue, Borno, Cross-River, Gongola, Kaduna, Kano, Lagos, Plateau, Rivers and Sokoto, in admission into federal universities (Ike 1986). Nine of these are from the north. Also because the definition of locality was not included in the application requirements or guidelines as it is now (see JAMB Brochure 2005/2006), it could have had the unstated purpose of restricting the chance of being admitted by the available choices. With the initial advantage from the location of a federal university that cannot be ignored as the Oyo example above cited, it is doubtful that JAMB has served as an instrument in helping ELD states to catch up with the educationally developed states. In 2000, the government cancelled the discretion criterion on account of its perceived abuse and fueling of violent cult activities in the universities. Thus, the criteria are currently: merit (45 per cent), locality (35 per cent), and ELD (20 per cent) (Salim 2003). The ongoing struggle by the universities to conduct a post-JAMB test for the purpose of admissions is likely to render impotent the guidelines if it succeeds.

As tables 4.10-4.20 show, the South-West (Zone 1) consistently had the largest enrolment with several thousands over the zone with the second largest enrolment in most of the years. The South-East (Zone 2) was in second position in the academic years 1980/81, 1981/82 and 1982/83 while the South-South (Zone 6) trailed closely behind in third position until the 1983/84 academic session when it pushed the South-East into third place. The South-East regained second position in the 1984/85 session, retaining it until the South-South again displaced it and stayed in second position through the 1990/91 and 1991/92 sessions, when available data ended. All the three northern zones, North-Central (Zone 5), North-East (Zone 4) and North-West (Zone 3) persistently fell behind the three southern zones in enrolment. They maintained constant positions in the order of fourth (North-Central), fifth (North-West) and sixth (North-East). The North-Central's enrolments are little more or less than the sum of the enrolments of the North-West and the North-East for each session.

As shown in Table 4.21, the northern enrolment figures increased steadily in relation to those of the south for four consecutive academic years, that is, between 1980/81 and 1984/85. It dropped very slightly in the 1985/86 session and fluctuated thereafter between the 1986/87 session and the 1990/91 session, reaching the highest-ever peak in the 1991/92 session. The analysis of the 1992/93 academic session to-date when completed is likely to present a more startling distribution of enrolments among zones, particularly the South-South's position in relation to the South-East and then in relation to the South-West; and the north's enrolments in relation to the south's as to steady increase or decrease.

The causes of the rises in northern enrolments from the 1980/81 session to the 1984/85 session are hard to find. From Table 4.21, the increase was about 0.7 per cent each year between the 1980/81 session and the 1982/83 session. It leaped to 1.9 per cent in the 1983/84 session. It seems reasonable then to conclude that the quota principle introduced into admissions by President Shehu Shagari's administration and first applied in the 1983/84 academic session helped to step up northern enrolment figures fairly well by about 2 per cent in the 1983/84 session. It fell to 0.8 per cent in the 1984/85 session and fluctuated thereafter as noted earlier until it rose from the previous year by 2.5 per cent in the 1991/92 session.

## Table 4.10: Enrolment into Federal Universities, Academic Year 1980/81

| S/No. | University | Zone 1 | | | Zone 2 | | | Zone 3 | | | Zone 4 | | | Zone 5 | | | Zone 6 | | | Total | | |
|---|---|---|---|---|---|---|---|---|---|---|---|---|---|---|---|---|---|---|---|---|---|---|
| | | M | F | Total | M | F | Total | M | F | Total | M | F | Total | M | F | Total | M | F | Total | M | F | Total |
| 1. | Ibadan | 3101 | 950 | 4051 | 930 | 254 | 1184 | 11 | – | 11 | 14 | – | 14 | 622 | 96 | 718 | 1249 | 315 | 1564 | 5927 | 1615 | 7542 |
| 2. | Lagos | 2912 | 974 | 3886 | 1144 | 319 | 1463 | 10 | 2 | 12 | 16 | – | 16 | 414 | 62 | 476 | 1688 | 417 | 2159 | 6184 | 1828 | 8012 |
| 3. | Nsukka | 568 | 69 | 637 | 6798 | 1389 | 8187 | 7 | 1 | 8 | 8 | – | 8 | 173 | 7 | 180 | 1099 | 128 | 1227 | 8663 | 1584 | 10247 |
| 4. | Zaria | 411 | 158 | 569 | 273 | 132 | 405 | 2395 | 334 | 2729 | 1508 | 214 | 1722 | 3241 | 748 | 3989 | 419 | 193 | 612 | 8247 | 1779 | 10026 |
| 5. | Ife | 5457 | 1905 | 7362 | 784 | 198 | 982 | 10 | 0 | 10 | 6 | 0 | 6 | 208 | 51 | 269 | 1049 | 323 | 1372 | 7524 | 2477 | 10001 |
| 6. | Benin | 559 | 201 | 760 | 918 | 497 | 1415 | 12 | 6 | 18 | 7 | 0 | 7 | 128 | 50 | 178 | 2220 | 1330 | 3550 | 3854 | 2074 | 5928 |
| 7. | Jos | 227 | 31 | 258 | 460 | 157 | 617 | 54 | 9 | 63 | 245 | 37 | 282 | 1164 | 203 | 1367 | 319 | 118 | 437 | 2469 | 555 | 3024 |
| 8. | Calabar | 140 | 29 | 169 | 387 | 91 | 478 | 15 | 3 | 18 | 4 | 0 | 4 | 71 | 17 | 88 | 1639 | 387 | 2029 | 2256 | 527 | 2783 |
| 9. | Kano | 55 | 19 | 74 | 23 | 14 | 37 | 1260 | 141 | 1401 | 416 | 48 | 464 | 400 | 53 | 453 | 28 | 10 | 38 | 2182 | 285 | 2467 |
| 10. | Maiduguri | 113 | 34 | 147 | 111 | 36 | 147 | 66 | 12 | 78 | 1538 | 178 | 1716 | 203 | 32 | 235 | 148 | 71 | 219 | 2179 | 363 | 2542 |
| 11. | Sokoto | 24 | 6 | 30 | 27 | 4 | 31 | 393 | 37 | 430 | 88 | 4 | 92 | 212 | 42 | 254 | 36 | 9 | 45 | 780 | 102 | 882 |
| 12. | Ilorin | 628 | 151 | 779 | 230 | 35 | 265 | 3 | 0 | 3 | 6 | 0 | 6 | 640 | 116 | 756 | 153 | 40 | 193 | 1660 | 342 | 2002 |
| 13. | Port Harcourt | 71 | 9 | 80 | 424 | 424 | 113 | 537 | 1 | 0 | 1 | 1 | 0 | 1 | 51 | 1 | 52 | 1113 | 1291 | 1661 | 301 | 1962 |
| | Total | 14266 | 4536 | 18802 | 12509 | 3239 | 15748 | 4237 | 545 | 4782 | 3857 | 481 | 4338 | 7537 | 1478 | 9015 | 11170 | 3563 | 14733 | 53576 | 13842 | 67418 |

Source: *National Universities Commission Statistical Digest 1980/81-1985/86*, Lagos: National Universities Commission, 1989.

## Table 4.11: Enrolment into Federal Universities, Academic Year 1981/82

| S/No. | University | Zone 1 | | | Zone 2 | | | Zone 3 | | | Zone 4 | | | Zone 5 | | | Zone 6 | | | Total | | |
|---|---|---|---|---|---|---|---|---|---|---|---|---|---|---|---|---|---|---|---|---|---|---|
| | | M | F | Total | M | F | Total | M | F | Total | M | F | Total | M | F | Total | M | F | Total | M | F | Total |
| 1. | Ibadan | 4333 | 1173 | 5506 | 927 | 253 | 1180 | 26 | 10 | 36 | 16 | 2 | 18 | 748 | 96 | 844 | 1472 | 312 | 1784 | 7522 | 1846 | 9368 |
| 2. | Lagos | 3470 | 1218 | 4688 | 904 | 340 | 1244 | 11 | 3 | 14 | 4 | 3 | 7 | 409 | 42 | 451 | 1550 | 460 | 2010 | 6348 | 2066 | 8414 |
| 3. | Nsukka | 548 | 82 | 630 | 7519 | 1957 | 9476 | 7 | 1 | 8 | 8 | 1 | 9 | 169 | 8 | 177 | 1070 | 152 | 1222 | 9321 | 2201 | 11522 |
| 4. | Zaria | 463 | 343 | 806 | 236 | 339 | 575 | 3212 | 672 | 3884 | 1752 | 373 | 2125 | 4172 | 1100 | 5272 | 488 | 455 | 943 | 10323 | 3282 | 13605 |
| 5. | Ife | 6601 | 2512 | 9113 | 653 | 242 | 895 | 14 | 0 | 14 | 6 | 0 | 6 | 197 | 70 | 267 | 1087 | 411 | 1498 | 8558 | 3245 | 11793 |
| 6. | Benin | 683 | 337 | 1020 | 1120 | 550 | 1670 | 14 | 3 | 17 | 17 | 8 | 25 | 103 | 23 | 126 | 2598 | 1549 | 4147 | 4535 | 2470 | 7005 |
| 7. | Jos | 280 | 69 | 349 | 616 | 142 | 758 | 86 | 20 | 106 | 415 | 34 | 449 | 1297 | 307 | 1604 | 359 | 150 | 509 | 3063 | 722 | 3775 |
| 8. | Calabar | 205 | 53 | 258 | 672 | 170 | 842 | 7 | 2 | 9 | 3 | 0 | 3 | 92 | 23 | 115 | 2115 | 536 | 2651 | 3094 | 784 | 3878 |
| 9. | Kano | 61 | 10 | 71 | 17 | 15 | 32 | 1378 | 134 | 1512 | 433 | 53 | 486 | 455 | 62 | 517 | 37 | 19 | 56 | 2381 | 293 | 2674 |
| 10. | Maiduguri | 142 | 52 | 194 | 137 | 86 | 223 | 86 | 15 | 101 | 1263 | 240 | 1503 | 263 | 47 | 310 | 213 | 86 | 299 | 2104 | 526 | 2630 |
| 11. | Sokoto | 28 | 1 | 29 | 54 | 11 | 65 | 577 | 30 | 607 | 105 | 22 | 127 | 262 | 14 | 276 | 53 | 11 | 64 | 1079 | 89 | 1168 |
| 12. | Ilorin | 821 | 240 | 1061 | 225 | 53 | 278 | 8 | 0 | 8 | 8 | 0 | 8 | 1030 | 164 | 1194 | 170 | 55 | 225 | 2262 | 512 | 2774 |
| 13. | PortHarcourt | 82 | 14 | 96 | 526 | 135 | 661 | 0 | 0 | 0 | 2 | 0 | 2 | 65 | 3 | 68 | 1405 | 242 | 1647 | 2080 | 394 | 2474 |
| 14. | Bauchi | 35 | 14 | 49 | 32 | 19 | 51 | 7 | 1 | 8 | 54 | 9 | 63 | 35 | 5 | 40 | 36 | 13 | 49 | 199 | 61 | 260 |
| 15. | Makurdi | 25 | 4 | 29 | 22 | 1 | 23 | 3 | 0 | 3 | 4 | 0 | 4 | 109 | 2 | 111 | 25 | 1 | 26 | 188 | 8 | 196 |
| 16. | Oweni | 18 | 2 | 20 | 107 | 16 | 123 | 2 | 0 | 2 | 0 | 0 | 0 | 14 | 1 | 15 | 63 | 8 | 71 | 204 | 27 | 231 |
| | Total | 17795 | 6124 | 23919 | 13767 | 4329 | 18096 | 5438 | 891 | 6329 | 4090 | 745 | 4835 | 9420 | 1967 | 11387 | 12741 | 4460 | 17201 | 63251 | 18516 | 81767 |

Source: *National Universities Commission Statistical Digest 1980/81-1985/86,* Lagos: National Universities Commission, 1989.

## Table 4.12: Enrolment into Federal Universities, Academic Year 1982/83

| S/No. | University | Zone 1 | | | Zone 2 | | | Zone 3 | | | Zone 4 | | | Zone 5 | | | Zone 6 | | | Total | | |
|---|---|---|---|---|---|---|---|---|---|---|---|---|---|---|---|---|---|---|---|---|---|---|
| | | M | F | Total | M | F | Total | M | F | Total | M | F | Total | M | F | Total | M | F | Total | M | F | Total |
| 1 | Ibadan | 5,048 | 1,429 | 6,477 | 1,011 | 132 | 1,143 | 29 | 5 | 34 | 17 | 13 | 30 | 915 | 120 | 1,035 | 1,655 | 433 | 2,088 | 8,675 | 2,132 | 10,807 |
| 2 | Lagos | 3,838 | 1,381 | 5,209 | 897 | 374 | 1,271 | 10 | 5 | 15 | 12 | 4 | 16 | 353 | 41 | 394 | 1,534 | 471 | 2,005 | 6,634 | 2,276 | 8,910 |
| 3 | Nsukka | 522 | 70 | 592 | 8,250 | 2,319 | 10,569 | 18 | 0 | 18 | 26 | 0 | 26 | 173 | 18 | 191 | 1,192 | 158 | 1,350 | 10,181 | 2,565 | 12,746 |
| 4 | Zaria | 527 | 244 | 771 | 394 | 193 | 587 | 3,268 | 468 | 3,736 | 2,019 | 300 | 2,319 | 3,817 | 853 | 4,670 | 503 | 263 | 766 | 10,528 | 2,321 | 12,849 |
| 5 | Ife | 5,107 | 3,738 | 8,845 | 568 | 456 | 1,024 | 0 | 0 | 0 | 6 | 0 | 6 | 173 | 71 | 244 | 768 | 524 | 1,292 | 6,622 | 4,789 | 11,411 |
| 6 | Benin | 604 | 329 | 933 | 1,268 | 634 | 1,902 | 24 | 10 | 34 | 52 | 4 | 56 | 182 | 78 | 260 | 3,238 | 1,823 | 5,061 | 5,368 | 2,878 | 8,246 |
| 7 | Jos | 294 | 82 | 376 | 468 | 184 | 652 | 71 | 22 | 93 | 321 | 57 | 378 | 1,628 | 306 | 1,934 | 432 | 145 | 577 | 3,214 | 796 | 4,010 |
| 8 | Calabar | 182 | 45 | 227 | 771 | 252 | 1,023 | 22 | 3 | 25 | 5 | 1 | 6 | 89 | 113 | 202 | 2,249 | 657 | 2,906 | 3,318 | 1,071 | 4,289 |
| 9 | Kano | 73 | 17 | 90 | 20 | 19 | 39 | 1,730 | 193 | 1,923 | 453 | 56 | 509 | 578 | 73 | 651 | 57 | 22 | 79 | 2,911 | 380 | 3,291 |
| 10 | Maiduguri | 128 | 61 | 189 | 160 | 111 | 271 | 96 | 10 | 106 | 1,899 | 371 | 2,270 | 262 | 64 | 326 | 172 | 92 | 264 | 2,717 | 709 | 3,426 |
| 11 | Sokoto | 42 | 10 | 52 | 38 | 22 | 60 | 903 | 84 | 987 | 108 | 9 | 117 | 524 | 54 | 578 | 60 | 29 | 89 | 1,675 | 208 | 1,883 |
| 12 | Ilorin | 1,207 | 330 | 1,537 | 248 | 78 | 326 | 9 | 1 | 10 | 12 | 1 | 13 | 1,549 | 258 | 1,807 | 255 | 68 | 323 | 3,280 | 736 | 4,016 |
| 13 | Port Harcourt | 88 | 19 | 107 | 529 | 168 | 697 | 0 | 0 | 0 | 1 | 0 | 1 | 61 | 5 | 66 | 1,639 | 308 | 1,947 | 2,318 | 500 | 2,818 |
| 14 | Bauchi | 87 | 22 | 109 | 61 | 29 | 90 | 37 | 2 | 39 | 76 | 12 | 88 | 80 | 11 | 91 | 67 | 19 | 86 | 408 | 95 | 503 |
| 15 | Makurdi | 43 | 5 | 48 | 44 | 7 | 51 | 9 | 0 | 9 | 9 | 0 | 9 | 150 | 11 | 161 | 43 | 3 | 46 | 298 | 26 | 324 |
| 16 | Owerri | 31 | 5 | 36 | 187 | 17 | 204 | 1 | 0 | 1 | 1 | 0 | 1 | 24 | 1 | 25 | 89 | 6 | 95 | 333 | 29 | 362 |
| 17 | Akure | 83 | 13 | 96 | 11 | 2 | 13 | 0 | 0 | 0 | 0 | 0 | 0 | 5 | 0 | 5 | 30 | 5 | 35 | 129 | 20 | 149 |
| 18 | Yola | 3 | 1 | 4 | 45 | 7 | 52 | 0 | 0 | 0 | 42 | 3 | 45 | 9 | 1 | 10 | 11 | 4 | 15 | 110 | 16 | 126 |
| | Total | 17,897 | 7,801 | 25,698 | 14,970 | 5,004 | 19,974 | 6,227 | 803 | 7,030 | 5,059 | 831 | 5,890 | 10,572 | 2,078 | 12,650 | 13,394 | 5,030 | 19,024 | 68,719 | 21,547 | 90,266 |

Source: *National Universities Commission Statistical Digest 1980/81-1985/86*, Lagos: National Universities Commission, 1989.

## Table 4.13: Enrolment into Federal Universities, Academic Year 1983/84

| S/No | University | Zone 1 | | | Zone 2 | | | Zone 3 | | | Zone 4 | | | Zone 5 | | | Zone 6 | | | Total | | |
|---|---|---|---|---|---|---|---|---|---|---|---|---|---|---|---|---|---|---|---|---|---|---|
| | | M | F | Total | M | F | Total | M | F | Total | M | F | Total | M | F | Total | M | F | Total | M | F | Total |
| 1. | Ibadan | 5313 | 1845 | 7158 | 948 | 340 | 1288 | 24 | 1 | 25 | 42 | 0 | 42 | 895 | 106 | 1001 | 1767 | 540 | 2307 | 8989 | 2832 | 11821 |
| 2. | Lagos | 4196 | 1429 | 5625 | 1003 | 388 | 1391 | 13 | 0 | 13 | 12 | 4 | 16 | 297 | 44 | 341 | 1386 | 450 | 1836 | 6007 | 2315 | 9222 |
| 3. | Nsukka | 449 | 46 | 495 | 8293 | 2228 | 10521 | 15 | 2 | 17 | 32 | 0 | 32 | 181 | 7 | 188 | 1184 | 121 | 1305 | 10054 | 2404 | 12458 |
| 4. | Zaria | 476 | 212 | 688 | 365 | 200 | 565 | 3783 | 560 | 4343 | 2268 | 334 | 2602 | 4066 | 980 | 5046 | 443 | 231 | 674 | 11401 | 2517 | 13918 |
| 5. | Ife | 6968 | 2593 | 9561 | 385 | 158 | 543 | 20 | 0 | 20 | 13 | 0 | 13 | 183 | 47 | 230 | 863 | 277 | 1140 | 8432 | 3075 | 11507 |
| 6. | Benin | 916 | 299 | 1215 | 1141 | 467 | 1608 | 26 | 9 | 35 | 16 | 6 | 22 | 171 | 43 | 214 | 4258 | 1438 | 5696 | 6528 | 2262 | 8790 |
| 7. | Jos | 322 | 76 | 398 | 536 | 226 | 762 | 89 | 19 | 108 | 332 | 44 | 376 | 1941 | 357 | 2298 | 403 | 149 | 552 | 3623 | 871 | 4494 |
| 8. | Calabar | 193 | 25 | 218 | 868 | 330 | 1198 | 4 | 0 | 4 | 4 | 1 | 5 | 90 | 6 | 96 | 2235 | 869 | 3104 | 3394 | 1231 | 4625 |
| 9. | Kano | 51 | 16 | 67 | 20 | 17 | 37 | 2158 | 210 | 2368 | 458 | 56 | 514 | 634 | 64 | 698 | 30 | 23 | 64 | 3360 | 388 | 3748 |
| 10. | Maiduguri | 148 | 78 | 226 | 211 | 160 | 371 | 201 | 44 | 245 | 2473 | 828 | 3301 | 330 | 146 | 476 | 236 | 149 | 385 | 3599 | 1405 | 5004 |
| 11. | Sokoto | 47 | 19 | 66 | 57 | 33 | 90 | 1184 | 122 | 1306 | 116 | 9 | 125 | 670 | 77 | 747 | 73 | 33 | 106 | 2147 | 293 | 2440 |
| 12. | Ilorin | 1460 | 431 | 1891 | 223 | 81 | 304 | 10 | 1 | 11 | 14 | 1 | 15 | 1553 | 406 | 1959 | 264 | 78 | 342 | 3524 | 998 | 4522 |
| 13. | Port Harcourt | 84 | 19 | 103 | 537 | 162 | 699 | 1 | 0 | 1 | 2 | 0 | 2 | 48 | 6 | 54 | 2109 | 403 | 2432 | 2701 | 590 | 3291 |
| 14. | Bauchi | 94 | 16 | 110 | 162 | 22 | 184 | 21 | 1 | 22 | 231 | 2 | 233 | 82 | 5 | 87 | 102 | 11 | 113 | 692 | 57 | 749 |
| 15. | Makurdi | 66 | 11 | 77 | 59 | 13 | 72 | 10 | 0 | 10 | 7 | 0 | 7 | 202 | 11 | 213 | 56 | 8 | 64 | 400 | 43 | 443 |
| 16. | Owerri | 41 | 3 | 44 | 257 | 26 | 283 | 1 | 0 | 1 | 0 | 0 | 0 | 24 | 1 | 25 | 96 | 7 | 103 | 419 | 37 | 456 |
| 17. | Akure | 213 | 21 | 234 | 13 | 0 | 13 | 0 | 0 | 0 | 0 | 0 | 0 | 13 | 0 | 13 | 30 | 5 | 35 | 269 | 26 | 295 |
| 18. | Yola | 7 | 0 | 7 | 74 | 14 | 88 | 1 | 0 | 1 | 76 | 14 | 90 | 11 | 1 | 12 | 19 | 2 | 21 | 188 | 31 | 219 |
| 19. | Abeokuta | 130 | 29 | 159 | 29 | 5 | 34 | 1 | 0 | 1 | 1 | 0 | 1 | 4 | 0 | 4 | 33 | 2 | 35 | 198 | 36 | 234 |
| 20. | Minna | 3 | 2 | 5 | 28 | 6 | 34 | 0 | 0 | 0 | 1 | 0 | 1 | 50 | 11 | 61 | 25 | 5 | 30 | 107 | 24 | 131 |
| | Total | 21177 | 7170 | 28347 | 15209 | 4876 | 20085 | 7562 | 969 | 8531 | 6198 | 1299 | 7397 | 11445 | 2318 | 13763 | 15441 | 4803 | 20244 | 76932 | 21435 | 98367 |

Source: *National Universities Commission Statistical Digest 1980/81-1985/86*, Lagos: National Universities Commission, 1989.

## Table 4.14: Enrolment into Federal Universities, Academic Year 1984/85

| S/No. | University | Zone 1 M | Zone 1 F | Zone 1 Total | Zone 2 M | Zone 2 F | Zone 2 Total | Zone 3 M | Zone 3 F | Zone 3 Total | Zone 4 M | Zone 4 F | Zone 4 Total | Zone 5 M | Zone 5 F | Zone 5 Total | Zone 6 M | Zone 6 F | Zone 6 Total | Total M | Total F | Total |
|---|---|---|---|---|---|---|---|---|---|---|---|---|---|---|---|---|---|---|---|---|---|---|
| 1. | Ibadan | 6,323 | 1,533 | 7,856 | 1,204 | 423 | 1,627 | 32 | 3 | 35 | 12 | 1 | 13 | 919 | 108 | 1,027 | 1,891 | 556 | 2,447 | 10,381 | 2,624 | 13,005 |
| 2. | Lagos | 4,460 | 1,684 | 6,144 | 953 | 403 | 1,356 | 15 | 3 | 18 | 12 | 2 | 14 | 262 | 30 | 312 | 1,355 | 501 | 1,856 | 7,057 | 2,643 | 9,700 |
| 3. | Abeokuta | 157 | 51 | 208 | 32 | 4 | 36 | 2 | 0 | 2 | 0 | 0 | 0 | 5 | 0 | 5 | 44 | 8 | 52 | 240 | 63 | 303 |
| 4. | Nsukka | 410 | 33 | 443 | 8,262 | 2,290 | 10,552 | 13 | 1 | 14 | 30 | 30 | 1 | 31 | 179 | 14 | 193 | 123 | 1,114 | 9,885 | 2,462 | 12,347 |
| 5. | Zaria | 484 | 262 | 746 | 256 | 292 | 548 | 3,905 | 657 | 4,542 | 2,335 | 347 | 2,682 | 4,378 | 1,131 | 5,509 | 396 | 354 | 750 | 11,754 | 3,023 | 14,777 |
| 6. | Bauchi | 74 | 10 | 84 | 280 | 34 | 314 | 87 | 2 | 89 | 130 | 7 | 137 | 139 | 8 | 167 | 202 | 17 | 219 | 932 | 78 | 1,010 |
| 7. | Ife | 7,204 | 2,635 | 9,839 | 491 | 186 | 677 | 12 | 11 | 23 | 15 | 14 | 19 | 240 | 58 | 298 | 888 | 278 | 1,164 | 8,848 | 3,172 | 12,020 |
| 8. | Benin | 919 | 326 | 1,245 | 1,188 | 585 | 1,773 | 39 | 9 | 48 | 16 | 9 | 25 | 173 | 37 | 210 | 4,730 | 1,597 | 6,327 | 7,065 | 2,563 | 9,628 |
| 9. | Jos | 434 | 116 | 550 | 609 | 283 | 892 | 39 | 8 | 67 | 330 | 53 | 383 | 2,066 | 410 | 2,476 | 476 | 195 | 671 | 3,874 | 1,065 | 5,039 |
| 10. | Makurdi | 73 | 11 | 84 | 83 | 20 | 103 | 9 | 0 | 9 | 12 | 0 | 12 | 266 | 29 | 295 | 75 | 11 | 86 | 518 | 71 | 589 |
| 11. | Calabar | 158 | 29 | 187 | 946 | 370 | 1,316 | 9 | 0 | 9 | 1 | 1 | 2 | 79 | 4 | 83 | 2,378 | 866 | 3,244 | 3,571 | 1,270 | 4,841 |
| 12. | Kano | 52 | 17 | 70 | 52 | 18 | 70 | 2,417 | 265 | 2,682 | 504 | 45 | 549 | 620 | 72 | 692 | 58 | 19 | 77 | 3,674 | 436 | 4,110 |
| 13. | Maiduguri | 176 | 103 | 279 | 250 | 168 | 418 | 211 | 118 | 329 | 3,048 | 907 | 3,955 | 371 | 195 | 566 | 232 | 157 | 389 | 4,288 | 1,648 | 5,936 |
| 14. | Yola | 6 | 2 | 8 | 27 | 10 | 37 | 1 | 0 | 1 | 88 | 10 | 98 | 2 | 1 | 3 | 7 | 2 | 9 | 126 | 25 | 151 |
| 15. | Sokoto | 68 | 13 | 81 | 59 | 16 | 75 | 1,646 | 142 | 1,788 | 145 | 13 | 158 | 941 | 110 | 1,051 | 84 | 35 | 119 | 2,943 | 329 | 3,272 |
| 16. | Ilorin | 1,769 | 538 | 2,307 | 266 | 76 | 342 | 14 | 1 | 15 | 17 | 1 | 18 | 1,933 | 423 | 2,356 | 203 | 91 | 384 | 4,252 | 1,130 | 5,382 |
| 17. | Port Harcourt | 114 | 20 | 134 | 851 | 309 | 1,160 | 2 | 0 | 2 | 2 | 0 | 2 | 54 | 5 | 59 | 1,995 | 417 | 2,412 | 3,018 | 751 | 3,769 |
| 18. | Owerri | 49 | 2 | 51 | 444 | 43 | 487 | 1 | 0 | 1 | 1 | 0 | 1 | 22 | 1 | 23 | 119 | 6 | 125 | 636 | 52 | 688 |
| 19. | Akure | 246 | 28 | 274 | 47 | 5 | 52 | 1 | 0 | 1 | 0 | 0 | 0 | 17 | 0 | 17 | 62 | 6 | 68 | 373 | 39 | 412 |
| 20. | Minna | 18 | 3 | 21 | 34 | 9 | 43 | 8 | 3 | 11 | 5 | 1 | 6 | 159 | 23 | 182 | 29 | 10 | 39 | 253 | 49 | 302 |
| | Total | 23,195 | 7,416 | 30,611 | 16,264 | 5,544 | 21,808 | 8,483 | 2,103 | 9,686 | 6,698 | 1,402 | 8,100 | 12,945 | 2,679 | 15,524 | 16,303 | 5,249 | 21,552 | 83,788 | 23,493 | 107,281 |

Source: *National Universities Commission Statistical Digest 1980/81-1985/86*, Lagos: National Universities Commission, 1989.

## Table 4.15: Enrolment into Federal Universities, Academic Year 1985/86

| S/No | University | Zone 1 | | | Zone 2 | | | Zone 3 | | | Zone 4 | | | Zone 5 | | | Zone 6 | | | Total | | |
|---|---|---|---|---|---|---|---|---|---|---|---|---|---|---|---|---|---|---|---|---|---|---|
| | | M | F | Total | M | F | Total | M | F | Total | M | F | Total | M | F | Total | M | F | Total | M | F | Total |
| 1 | Ibadan | 5,729 | 2,042 | 7,771 | 932 | 375 | 1,307 | 34 | 3 | 37 | 31 | 12 | 43 | 728 | 107 | 835 | 1,582 | 541 | 2,123 | 9,036 | 3,080 | 12,116 |
| 2 | Lagos | 4,858 | 1,911 | 6,769 | 1,027 | 442 | 1,469 | 18 | 4 | 22 | 9 | 9 | 18 | 312 | 66 | 378 | 1,358 | 525 | 1,883 | 7,582 | 2,957 | 10,539 |
| 3 | Abeokuta | 217 | 71 | 288 | 27 | 9 | 36 | 1 | 0 | 1 | 0 | 0 | 0 | 12 | 0 | 12 | 59 | 15 | 74 | 316 | 95 | 411 |
| 4 | Nsukka | 378 | 51 | 429 | 8,243 | 2,382 | 10,625 | 23 | 2 | 25 | 30 | 0 | 30 | 191 | 15 | 206 | 960 | 157 | 1,117 | 9,825 | 2,607 | 12,432 |
| 5 | Zaria | 491 | 228 | 719 | 323 | 246 | 569 | 3,892 | 596 | 4,488 | 2,319 | 317 | 2,636 | 4,440 | 1,111 | 5,551 | 411 | 244 | 655 | 11,876 | 2,742 | 14,618 |
| 6 | Bauchi | 78 | 11 | 89 | 96 | 27 | 123 | 41 | 3 | 44 | 130 | 19 | 149 | 150 | 11 | 161 | 68 | 14 | 82 | 563 | 85 | 648 |
| 7 | Ife | 7,428 | 2,465 | 9,893 | 485 | 163 | 648 | 7 | 5 | 12 | 11 | 1 | 12 | 245 | 58 | 303 | 896 | 265 | 1,161 | 9,072 | 2,957 | 12,029 |
| 8 | Benin | 970 | 314 | 1,284 | 1,312 | 572 | 1,884 | 49 | 12 | 61 | 49 | 14 | 63 | 182 | 40 | 222 | 4,396 | 1,574 | 5,970 | 6,958 | 2,526 | 9,484 |
| 9 | Jos | 403 | 131 | 534 | 655 | 375 | 1,030 | 137 | 15 | 152 | 387 | 88 | 475 | 2,084 | 427 | 2,511 | 495 | 250 | 745 | 4,161 | 1,286 | 5,447 |
| 10 | Makurdi | 82 | 15 | 97 | 110 | 27 | 137 | 10 | 0 | 10 | 36 | 4 | 40 | 389 | 52 | 441 | 72 | 14 | 86 | 699 | 112 | 811 |
| 11 | Calabar | 100 | 30 | 130 | 1,044 | 421 | 1,465 | 8 | 1 | 9 | 7 | 0 | 7 | 72 | 7 | 79 | 2,133 | 825 | 2,958 | 3,364 | 1,284 | 4,648 |
| 12 | Kano | 38 | 15 | 53 | 24 | 19 | 43 | 2,612 | 315 | 2,927 | 468 | 43 | 511 | 536 | 74 | 610 | 52 | 24 | 76 | 3,730 | 490 | 4,220 |
| 13 | Maiduguri | 194 | 79 | 273 | 313 | 201 | 514 | 144 | 33 | 177 | 2,938 | 756 | 3,694 | 344 | 114 | 458 | 223 | 167 | 390 | 4,156 | 1,350 | 5,506 |
| 14 | Yola | 10 | 3 | 13 | 37 | 9 | 46 | 2 | 0 | 2 | 133 | 19 | 156 | 7 | 3 | 10 | 9 | 4 | 13 | 198 | 38 | 236 |
| 15 | Sokoto | 68 | 37 | 105 | 66 | 34 | 99 | 1,985 | 215 | 2,200 | 125 | 11 | 136 | 834 | 99 | 933 | 98 | 39 | 137 | 3,175 | 435 | 3,610 |
| 16 | Ilorin | 1,984 | 695 | 2,679 | 183 | 78 | 261 | 12 | 4 | 16 | 16 | 8 | 24 | 1,943 | 501 | 2,444 | 301 | 92 | 393 | 4,439 | 1,378 | 5,817 |
| 17 | Port Harcourt | 126 | 36 | 162 | 1,086 | 505 | 1,591 | 4 | 0 | 4 | 4 | 0 | 4 | 45 | 6 | 51 | 2,156 | 529 | 2,685 | 3,421 | 1,076 | 4,497 |
| 18 | Owerri | 71 | 5 | 76 | 668 | 65 | 733 | 1 | 0 | 1 | 3 | 0 | 3 | 28 | 1 | 29 | 155 | 8 | 163 | 926 | 79 | 1,005 |
| 19 | Akure | 384 | 51 | 435 | 63 | 7 | 70 | 1 | 0 | 1 | 0 | 0 | 0 | 20 | 1 | 21 | 88 | 8 | 96 | 556 | 67 | 623 |
| 20 | Minna | 39 | 7 | 46 | 45 | 14 | 59 | 17 | 5 | 22 | 11 | 1 | 12 | 205 | 29 | 234 | 42 | 11 | 53 | 359 | 67 | 426 |
| | Total | 23,648 | 8,197 | 31,845 | 16,738 | 5,971 | 22,709 | 8,998 | 1,213 | 10,211 | 6,707 | 1,302 | 8,009 | 12,767 | 2,722 | 15,489 | 15,554 | 5,306 | 20,860 | 84,412 | 24,711 | 109,123 |

Source: *National Universities Commission Statistical Digest 1980/81-1985/86*, Lagos: National Universities Commission, 1989.

## Table 4.16: Enrolment into Federal Universities, Academic Year 1986/87

| S/No. | University | Zone 1 | | | Zone 2 | | | Zone 3 | | | Zone 4 | | | Zone 5 | | | Zone 6 | | | Total | | |
|---|---|---|---|---|---|---|---|---|---|---|---|---|---|---|---|---|---|---|---|---|---|---|
| | | M | F | Total | M | F | Total | M | F | Total | M | F | Total | M | F | Total | M | F | Total | M | F | Total |
| 1 | Ibadan | 5,832 | 2,212 | 8,044 | 722 | 321 | 1,043 | 29 | 3 | 32 | 24 | 1 | 25 | 666 | 121 | 787 | 1,321 | 511 | 1,832 | 8,594 | 3,169 | 11,763 |
| 2 | Lagos | 5,264 | 2,161 | 7,425 | 1,054 | 505 | 1,559 | 16 | 13 | 29 | 21 | 8 | 29 | 372 | 78 | 450 | 1,535 | 557 | 2,092 | 8,262 | 3,322 | 11,584 |
| 3 | Abeokuta | 342 | 107 | 449 | 41 | 10 | 51 | 0 | 0 | 0 | 0 | 0 | 0 | 17 | 1 | 18 | 66 | 17 | 83 | 466 | 135 | 601 |
| 4 | Nsukka | 475 | 67 | 542 | 6,682 | 2,724 | 9,406 | 34 | 5 | 39 | 37 | 4 | 41 | 229 | 32 | 261 | 1,068 | 176 | 1,234 | 8,515 | 308 | 11,523 |
| 5 | Zaria | 464 | 210 | 674 | 311 | 234 | 545 | 3,770 | 584 | 4,354 | 2,170 | 364 | 2,534 | 4,310 | 1,138 | 5,448 | 384 | 229 | 613 | 11,409 | 2,759 | 14,168 |
| 6 | Bauchi | 133 | 21 | 154 | 113 | 36 | 149 | 79 | 14 | 93 | 209 | 25 | 234 | 211 | 35 | 246 | 86 | 21 | 107 | 831 | 152 | 983 |
| 7 | Ife | 8,626 | 2,595 | 11,221 | 481 | 156 | 637 | 18 | 2 | 20 | 20 | 1 | 21 | 255 | 50 | 305 | 1,037 | 263 | 1,300 | 10,437 | 3,067 | 13,504 |
| 8 | Benin | 1,327 | 520 | 1,847 | 1,751 | 735 | 2,486 | 127 | 42 | 169 | 86 | 20 | 106 | 330 | 121 | 451 | 3,812 | 1,486 | 5,298 | 7,433 | 2,924 | 13,281 |
| 9 | Jos | 448 | 194 | 642 | 656 | 449 | 1,105 | 149 | 35 | 184 | 362 | 69 | 431 | 2,043 | 582 | 2,625 | 455 | 277 | 772 | 4,153 | 1,606 | 5,759 |
| 10 | Makurdi | 82 | 16 | 98 | 113 | 35 | 148 | 10 | 0 | 10 | 36 | 4 | 40 | 488 | 29 | 517 | 75 | 21 | 96 | 774 | 135 | 909 |
| 11 | Calabar | 100 | 30 | 130 | 1,044 | 421 | 1,465 | 8 | 0 | 8 | 7 | 1 | 8 | 72 | 7 | 79 | 2,567 | 875 | 3,442 | 3,798 | 1,334 | 5,132 |
| 12 | Kano | 45 | 18 | 63 | 24 | 21 | 45 | 2,681 | 375 | 3,056 | 422 | 50 | 472 | 473 | 78 | 551 | 40 | 20 | 60 | 3,685 | 562 | 4,247 |
| 13 | Maiduguri | 244 | 105 | 349 | 370 | 249 | 619 | 198 | 48 | 246 | 4,075 | 1,070 | 5,145 | 435 | 157 | 592 | 261 | 186 | 447 | 5,583 | 815 | 7,398 |
| 14 | Yola | 16 | 2 | 18 | 36 | 14 | 50 | 5 | 1 | 6 | 280 | 60 | 340 | 18 | 6 | 24 | 19 | 7 | 26 | 374 | 91 | 464 |
| 15 | Sokoto | 75 | 29 | 104 | 60 | 32 | 92 | 1,926 | 221 | 2,147 | 102 | 14 | 116 | 788 | 90 | 878 | 89 | 39 | 128 | 3,040 | 425 | 3,465 |
| 16 | Ilorin | 1,914 | 583 | 2,524 | 175 | 77 | 252 | 15 | 4 | 19 | 8 | 2 | 10 | 2,131 | 494 | 2,625 | 273 | 85 | 358 | 4,543 | 1,245 | 5,788 |
| 17 | Port Harcourt | 120 | 34 | 154 | 1,455 | 492 | 1,847 | 1 | 0 | 1 | 5 | 0 | 5 | 48 | 2 | 50 | 2,138 | 574 | 2,712 | 3,667 | 1,102 | 4,769 |
| 18 | Owerri | 79 | 3 | 82 | 886 | 78 | 964 | 4 | 0 | 4 | 2 | 0 | 2 | 26 | 0 | 26 | 186 | 12 | 198 | 1,183 | 93 | 1,276 |
| 19 | Akure | 557 | 91 | 648 | 80 | 11 | 91 | 1 | 0 | 1 | 0 | 0 | 0 | 28 | 1 | 29 | 121 | 13 | 134 | 787 | 116 | 903 |
| 20 | Minna | 48 | 23 | 71 | 55 | 12 | 67 | 33 | 4 | 37 | 17 | 1 | 18 | 268 | 34 | 302 | 54 | 17 | 71 | 475 | 91 | 566 |
| | Total | 26,218 | 9,021 | 35,239 | 16,009 | 6,612 | 22,621 | 9,104 | 1,351 | 10,455 | 7,883 | 1,694 | 9,577 | 13,178 | 3,086 | 16,264 | 15,617 | 5,386 | 21,003 | 88,009 | 27,150 | 115,159 |

Source: *National Universities Commission Statistical Digest 1988-1992*, Abuja: National Universities Commission, 1992

## Table 4.17: Enrolment into Federal Universities, Academic Year 1988/89

| S/No. | University | Zone 1 | | | Zone 2 | | | Zone 3 | | | Zone 4 | | | Zone 5 | | | Zone 6 | | | Total | | |
|---|---|---|---|---|---|---|---|---|---|---|---|---|---|---|---|---|---|---|---|---|---|---|
| | | M | F | Total | M | F | Total | M | F | Total | M | F | Total | M | F | Total | M | F | Total | M | F | Total |
| 1. | Ibadan | 5,624 | 2,214 | 7,838 | 782 | 318 | 1,100 | 46 | 8 | 54 | 53 | 5 | 58 | 691 | 157 | 848 | 1337 | 581 | 1,918 | 8,533 | 3,283 | 11,816 |
| 2. | Lagos | 7,162 | 2,834 | 9,996 | 2,236 | 845 | 3,081 | 60 | 11 | 71 | 47 | 20 | 67 | 661 | 182 | 843 | 2517 | 794 | 3,311 | 12,683 | 4,686 | 17,369 |
| 3. | Nsukka | 374 | 62 | 436 | 8,563 | 3,050 | 11,613 | 35 | 2 | 37 | 30 | 7 | 37 | 280 | 31 | 311 | 1178 | 194 | 1,372 | 10,460 | 3,346 | 13,806 |
| 4. | Zaria | 310 | 132 | 442 | 191 | 178 | 369 | 2,748 | 539 | 3,287 | 1,464 | 316 | 1,780 | 3,720 | 955 | 4,675 | 287 | 150 | 437 | 8,720 | 2,270 | 10,990 |
| 5. | Ife | 8,141 | 2,348 | 10,489 | 499 | 182 | 681 | 26 | 3 | 20 | 31 | 1 | 32 | 304 | 80 | 384 | 1,130 | 349 | 1,479 | 10,131 | 2,963 | 13,094 |
| 6. | Benin | 1,081 | 318 | 1,399 | 1,594 | 695 | 2,289 | 110 | 36 | 146 | 73 | 38 | 111 | 262 | 76 | 338 | 4,403 | 1,903 | 6,306 | 7,523 | 3,066 | 10,589 |
| 7. | Jos | 711 | 320 | 1,031 | 1,196 | 783 | 1,979 | 301 | 76 | 377 | 536 | 155 | 691 | 2,928 | 1,036 | 3,964 | 728 | 458 | 1,186 | 6,400 | 2,828 | 9,228 |
| 8. | Calabar | 118 | 28 | 146 | 1,128 | 427 | 1,555 | 7 | 1 | 8 | 7 | 0 | 7 | 155 | 37 | 192 | 2,343 | 366 | 3,209 | 3,758 | 1,359 | 5,117 |
| 9. | Kano | 57 | 21 | 78 | 33 | 24 | 57 | 3,172 | 439 | 3,611 | 408 | 80 | 488 | 633 | 121 | 754 | 62 | 32 | 94 | 4,365 | 717 | 5,082 |
| 10. | Maiduguri | 245 | 146 | 391 | 283 | 212 | 495 | 323 | 127 | 450 | 3,496 | 1,319 | 4,815 | 417 | 174 | 591 | 248 | 188 | 436 | 5,012 | 2,166 | 7,178 |
| 11. | Sokoto | 92 | 38 | 130 | 62 | 41 | 103 | 2,073 | 370 | 2,443 | 74 | 20 | 94 | 762 | 134 | 896 | 54 | 28 | 82 | 3,117 | 631 | 3,748 |
| 12. | Ilorin | 2,648 | 696 | 3,344 | 142 | 36 | 178 | 17 | 2 | 19 | 7 | 4 | 11 | 2,124 | 547 | 2,671 | 297 | 87 | 384 | 5,235 | 1,372 | 6,607 |
| 13. | Port Harcourt | 168 | 79 | 247 | 1,840 | 752 | 2,592 | 1 | 0 | 1 | 6 | 0 | 6 | 59 | 5 | 64 | 2,980 | 1,064 | 4,044 | 5,054 | 1,900 | 6,954 |
| 14. | Bauchi | 247 | 82 | 329 | 158 | 54 | 212 | 221 | 48 | 269 | 289 | 75 | 364 | 357 | 117 | 474 | 204 | 86 | 290 | 1,476 | 462 | 1,938 |
| 15. | Makurdi | 73 | 19 | 92 | 95 | 32 | 127 | 3 | 0 | 3 | 28 | 2 | 30 | 483 | 57 | 540 | 90 | 11 | 101 | 772 | 121 | 893 |
| 16. | Owerri | 87 | 7 | 94 | 1,303 | 167 | 1,470 | 4 | 0 | 4 | 1 | 0 | 1 | 32 | 0 | 32 | 283 | 29 | 312 | 1,710 | 203 | 1,913 |
| 17. | Yola | 39 | 7 | 46 | 19 | 12 | 31 | 82 | 6 | 88 | 435 | 82 | 517 | 35 | 14 | 49 | 27 | 19 | 46 | 637 | 140 | 777 |
| 18. | Akure | 854 | 144 | 998 | 82 | 13 | 95 | 2 | 1 | 3 | 1 | 0 | 1 | 35 | 1 | 36 | 152 | 20 | 172 | 1,126 | 179 | 1,305 |
| 19. | Abeokuta | 715 | 266 | 981 | 10 | 3 | 13 | 1 | 0 | 1 | 3 | 0 | 3 | 34 | 7 | 41 | 102 | 34 | 136 | 865 | 310 | 1,175 |
| 20. | Minna | 104 | 24 | 128 | 60 | 16 | 76 | 42 | 6 | 48 | 21 | 0 | 21 | 341 | 46 | 387 | 74 | 17 | 91 | 642 | 109 | 751 |
| | Total | 28,850 | 9,785 | 38,635 | 20,276 | 7,840 | 28,116 | 9,274 | 1675 | 10,949 | 7,010 | 2,124 | 9,134 | 14,313 | 3,777 | 18,090 | 18,496 | 6,910 | 25,406 | 98,219 | 32,111 | 130,330 |

Source: *National Universities Commission Statistical Digest 1988-1992*, Abuja: National Universities Commission, 1992

## Table 4.18: Enrolment into Federal Universities, Academic Year 1989/90

| S/No. | University | Zone 1 | | | Zone 2 | | | Zone 3 | | | Zone 4 | | | Zone 5 | | | Zone 6 | | | Total per School | | |
|---|---|---|---|---|---|---|---|---|---|---|---|---|---|---|---|---|---|---|---|---|---|---|
| | | M | F | Total | M | F | Total | M | F | Total | M | F | Total | M | F | Total | M | F | Total | M | F | Total |
| 1. | Ibadan | 5,892 | 2,281 | 8,173 | 686 | 318 | 1,004 | 57 | 9 | 66 | 55 | 3 | 58 | 668 | 156 | 814 | 1,353 | 547 | 1,900 | 8,791 | 3,314 | 12,015 |
| 2. | Lagos | 5,508 | 2,139 | 7,647 | 1,117 | 638 | 1,755 | 30 | 8 | 38 | 38 | 19 | 57 | 535 | 127 | 662 | 1,573 | 590 | 2,163 | 8,801 | 3,521 | 12,322 |
| 3. | Nsukka | 380 | 53 | 433 | 8,724 | 3,461 | 12,185 | 42 | 2 | 44 | 60 | 15 | 75 | 535 | 127 | 662 | 1,578 | 590 | 2,163 | 8,801 | 3,521 | 12,322 |
| 4. | Zaria | 310 | 132 | 442 | 191 | 178 | 369 | 2,748 | 539 | 3,287 | 1,464 | 316 | 1,780 | 3,720 | 955 | 4,675 | 287 | 150 | 437 | 8,720 | 2,270 | 10,990 |
| 5. | Ife | 8,687 | 2,432 | 11,119 | 581 | 199 | 780 | 30 | 3 | 33 | 37 | 1 | 38 | 362 | 84 | 446 | 1,272 | 364 | 1,636 | 10,969 | 3,083 | 14,052 |
| 6. | Benin | 1,327 | 647 | 1,974 | 1,349 | 587 | 1,936 | 240 | 135 | 375 | 144 | 92 | 236 | 537 | 241 | 778 | 3,630 | 1,894 | 5,524 | 7,227 | 3,596 | 10,823 |
| 7. | Jos | 697 | 316 | 1,013 | 1,091 | 685 | 1,776 | 365 | 89 | 454 | 566 | 138 | 704 | 3,402 | 1,087 | 4,489 | 754 | 421 | 1,175 | 6,875 | 2,736 | 9,611 |
| 8. | Calabar | 128 | 41 | 169 | 1,148 | 464 | 1,612 | 11 | 2 | 13 | 12 | 1 | 13 | 189 | 39 | 228 | 3,010 | 1,117 | 4,127 | 4,498 | 1,664 | 6,162 |
| 9. | Kano | 75 | 40 | 115 | 36 | 44 | 80 | 3,498 | 622 | 4,120 | 380 | 74 | 454 | 711 | 167 | 878 | 63 | 46 | 109 | 4,763 | 993 | 5,756 |
| 10. | Maiduguri | 206 | 92 | 298 | 159 | 122 | 281 | 247 | 51 | 298 | 4,399 | 1,226 | 5,625 | 293 | 126 | 419 | 139 | 101 | 240 | 5,443 | 1,718 | 7,161 |
| 11. | Sokoto | 100 | 35 | 135 | 77 | 41 | 118 | 2,198 | 346 | 2,544 | 76 | 19 | 95 | 875 | 146 | 1,021 | 68 | 27 | 95 | 3,394 | 614 | 4,008 |
| 12. | Ilorin | 2,946 | 787 | 3,733 | 156 | 49 | 205 | 12 | 1 | 13 | 22 | 0 | 22 | 2,422 | 729 | 3,151 | 383 | 96 | 479 | 5,941 | 1,662 | 7,603 |
| 13. | Port Harcourt | 209 | 68 | 277 | 2,019 | 1,014 | 3,033 | 6 | 1 | 6 | 13 | 0 | 13 | 83 | 7 | 90 | 3,102 | 1,172 | 4,274 | 5,432 | 2,261 | 7,693 |
| 14. | Bauchi | 172 | 52 | 224 | 162 | 32 | 194 | 202 | 53 | 255 | 408 | 107 | 515 | 476 | 126 | 602 | 172 | 48 | 220 | 1,592 | 418 | 2,010 |
| 15. | Makurdi | 107 | 22 | 129 | 94 | 36 | 130 | 3 | 0 | 3 | 24 | 1 | 25 | 538 | 72 | 610 | 101 | 21 | 122 | 867 | 152 | 1,019 |
| 16. | Owerri | 88 | 9 | 97 | 1,375 | 170 | 1,545 | 5 | 0 | 5 | 1 | 0 | 1 | 39 | 0 | 39 | 206 | 27 | 323 | 1,804 | 206 | 2,010 |
| 17. | Yola | 30 | 8 | 46 | 25 | 15 | 40 | 77 | 5 | 82 | 805 | 228 | 1,033 | 50 | 17 | 67 | 18 | 9 | 27 | 1,013 | 282 | 1,295 |
| 18. | Akure | 1,013 | 171 | 1,184 | 62 | 12 | 74 | 3 | 1 | 4 | 1 | 0 | 1 | 50 | 2 | 52 | 183 | 18 | 201 | 1,312 | 204 | 1,516 |
| 19. | Abeokuta | 683 | 228 | 911 | 53 | 18 | 71 | 1 | 0 | 1 | 9 | 1 | 10 | 37 | 10 | 47 | 100 | 36 | 136 | 883 | 293 | 1,176 |
| 20. | Minna | 148 | 32 | 180 | 78 | 21 | 99 | 149 | 21 | 170 | 89 | 5 | 94 | 567 | 94 | 661 | 113 | 25 | 138 | 1,144 | 198 | 1,342 |
| | Total Per Zone | 28,714 | 9,585 | 38,299 | 19,183 | 8,104 | 27,287 | 9,924 | 1,887 | 11,811 | 8,603 | 2,246 | 10,849 | 15,805 | 4,217 | 20,022 | 18,071 | 7,054 | 25,125 | 100,300 | 33,093 | 133,393 |

Source: *National Universities Commission Statistical Digest 1988-1992*, Abuja: National Universities Commission, 1992

## Table 4.19: Enrolment into Federal Universities, Academic Year 1990/91

| S/No. | University | Zone 1 M | Zone 1 F | Zone 1 Total | Zone 2 M | Zone 2 F | Zone 2 Total | Zone 3 M | Zone 3 F | Zone 3 Total | Zone 4 M | Zone 4 F | Zone 4 Total | Zone 5 M | Zone 5 F | Zone 5 Total | Zone 6 M | Zone 6 F | Zone 6 Total | Total Per School M | Total Per School F | Total Per School Total |
|---|---|---|---|---|---|---|---|---|---|---|---|---|---|---|---|---|---|---|---|---|---|---|
| 1. | Ibadan | 4,790 | 1,975 | 6,765 | 753 | 319 | 1,072 | 52 | 12 | 64 | 46 | 9 | 55 | 600 | 183 | 793 | 1,294 | 573 | 1,867 | 7,535 | 3,081 | 10,616 |
| 2. | Lagos | 5,527 | 2,139 | 7,666 | 1,117 | 638 | 1,755 | 35 | 8 | 43 | 42 | 19 | 61 | 534 | 127 | 662 | 1,573 | 590 | 2,163 | 8,829 | 3,521 | 12,350 |
| 3. | Nsukka | 360 | 59 | 419 | 9,243 | 3,809 | 13,052 | 66 | 7 | 73 | 42 | 15 | 57 | 345 | 38 | 383 | 1,528 | 312 | 1,840 | 11,584 | 4,240 | 15,824 |
| 4. | Zaria | 310 | 132 | 442 | 191 | 178 | 369 | 2,748 | 539 | 3,287 | 1,464 | 316 | 1,780 | 3,720 | 955 | 4,675 | 287 | 150 | 437 | 8,720 | 2,270 | 10,990 |
| 5. | Ife | 8,687 | 2,432 | 11,119 | 581 | 199 | 780 | 30 | 3 | 33 | 37 | 1 | 38 | 362 | 84 | 446 | 1,272 | 364 | 1,636 | 10,969 | 3,083 | 1,052 |
| 6. | Benin | 1,354 | 725 | 2,079 | 1,385 | 344 | 1,729 | 215 | 119 | 334 | 155 | 75 | 230 | 431 | 196 | 627 | 4,519 | 2,553 | 7,072 | 8,059 | 4,012 | 12,071 |
| 7. | Jos | 805 | 343 | 1,148 | 977 | 732 | 1,709 | 413 | 110 | 523 | 731 | 299 | 900 | 3,754 | 1,127 | 4,881 | 905 | 465 | 1,370 | 7,585 | 3,036 | 10,621 |
| 8. | Calabar | 209 | 55 | 264 | 1,344 | 678 | 2,022 | 19 | 2 | 21 | 30 | 1 | 31 | 294 | 77 | 371 | 3,544 | 1,413 | 4,957 | 5,440 | 2,226 | 7,666 |
| 9. | Kano | 155 | 60 | 215 | 109 | 24 | 133 | 3,972 | 810 | 4,782 | 540 | 80 | 620 | 634 | 120 | 754 | 132 | 28 | 160 | 5,542 | 1,122 | 6,664 |
| 10. | Maiduguri | 133 | 88 | 221 | 133 | 107 | 240 | 204 | 42 | 246 | 4,675 | 1,537 | 6,212 | 284 | 144 | 428 | 89 | 74 | 163 | 5,518 | 1,992 | 7,510 |
| 11. | Sokoto | 131 | 42 | 173 | 66 | 46 | 112 | 2,208 | 336 | 2,544 | 73 | 16 | 89 | 934 | 174 | 1,108 | 73 | 25 | 98 | 3,485 | 639 | 4,124 |
| 12. | Ilorin | 3,389 | 1,016 | 4,405 | 164 | 79 | 243 | 38 | 17 | 55 | 29 | 1 | 30 | 2,717 | 824 | 3,541 | 349 | 136 | 485 | 6,686 | 2,073 | 8,759 |
| 13. | Port Harcourt | 209 | 68 | 277 | 2,019 | 1,014 | 3,033 | 6 | 0 | 6 | 13 | 0 | 13 | 83 | 7 | 90 | 3,102 | 1,172 | 4,274 | 5,432 | 2,261 | 7,693 |
| 14. | Bauchi | 197 | 67 | 264 | 156 | 41 | 197 | 244 | 60 | 304 | 437 | 139 | 576 | 479 | 144 | 623 | 175 | 50 | 225 | 1,688 | 501 | 2,189 |
| 15. | Makurdi | 147 | 36 | 182 | 123 | 54 | 177 | 16 | 1 | 17 | 20 | 1 | 21 | 723 | 89 | 812 | 139 | 33 | 172 | 1,168 | 213 | 1,381 |
| 16. | Owerri | 94 | 12 | 106 | 1,633 | 229 | 1,862 | 3 | 0 | 3 | 1 | 0 | 1 | 39 | 0 | 39 | 379 | 28 | 407 | 2,149 | 269 | 2,418 |
| 17. | Yola | 67 | 15 | 82 | 39 | 17 | 56 | 102 | 6 | 108 | 1,083 | 119 | 1,202 | 110 | 22 | 132 | 41 | 18 | 59 | 1,442 | 197 | 1,639 |
| 18. | Akure | 1,239 | 207 | 1,446 | 73 | 17 | 90 | 0 | 0 | 0 | 2 | 0 | 2 | 64 | 3 | 67 | 212 | 28 | 240 | 1,590 | 255 | 1,845 |
| 19. | Abeokuta | 906 | 273 | 1,179 | 56 | 16 | 72 | 1 | 0 | 1 | 10 | 1 | 11 | 53 | 11 | 64 | 109 | 37 | 146 | 1,135 | 338 | 1,473 |
| 20. | Minna | 234 | 53 | 287 | 84 | 25 | 109 | 91 | 12 | 103 | 25 | 4 | 29 | 716 | 113 | 829 | 156 | 35 | 191 | 1,306 | 242 | 1,548 |
| 21. | Abuja | 14 | 18 | 32 | 13 | 16 | 29 | 17 | 20 | 37 | 17 | 11 | 28 | 32 | 30 | 62 | 13 | 22 | 35 | 106 | 117 | 223 |
| 22. | Uyo | 56 | 15 | 71 | 408 | 272 | 680 | 0 | 0 | 0 | 14 | 4 | 18 | 10 | 8 | 18 | 3,865 | 2,035 | 5,000 | 4,353 | 2,334 | 6,687 |
| | Total Per Zone | 29,013 | 9,829 | 38,842 | 20,667 | 8,854 | 29,521 | 10,480 | 2,104 | 12,584 | 9,486 | 2,608 | 12,094 | 16,919 | 4,486 | 21,405 | 23,756 | 10,141 | 33,897 | 110,321 | 38,022 | 148,343 |

Source: *National Universities Commission Statistical Digest 1988-1992*, Abuja: National Universities Commission, 1992

## Table 4.20: Enrolment into Federal Universities, Academic Year 1991/92

| S/No. | University | Zone 1 | | | Zone 2 | | | Zone 3 | | | Zone 4 | | | Zone 5 | | | Zone 6 | | | Total Per School | | |
|---|---|---|---|---|---|---|---|---|---|---|---|---|---|---|---|---|---|---|---|---|---|---|
| | | M | F | Total | M | F | Total | M | F | Total | M | F | Total | M | F | Total | M | F | Total | M | F | Total |
| 1. | Ibadan | 6,605 | 2,138 | 8,743 | 743 | 353 | 1,096 | 82 | 9 | 91 | 47 | 3 | 50 | 808 | 262 | 1,070 | 1,470 | 636 | 2,106 | 9,755 | 3,401 | 13,156 |
| 2. | Lagos | 5,568 | 2,478 | 8,046 | 1,347 | 819 | 2,166 | 57 | 13 | 70 | 58 | 22 | 80 | 638 | 78 | 716 | 1,774 | 826 | 2,600 | 9,442 | 4,236 | 13,678 |
| 3. | Nsukka | 378 | 71 | 449 | 9,610 | 5,205 | 14,815 | 123 | 29 | 152 | 88 | 10 | 98 | 484 | 67 | 551 | 1,858 | 437 | 2,295 | 12,541 | 5,819 | 18,360 |
| 4. | Zaria | 310 | 132 | 442 | 191 | 178 | 369 | 2,748 | 539 | 3,287 | 1,464 | 316 | 1,780 | 3,720 | 955 | 4,675 | 287 | 150 | 437 | 8,720 | 2,270 | 10,990 |
| 5. | Ife | 8,687 | 2,432 | 11,119 | 370 | 88 | 458 | 30 | 3 | 33 | 37 | 1 | 38 | 362 | 84 | 446 | 1,272 | 364 | 1,636 | 10,758 | 2,972 | 13,730 |
| 6. | Benin | 1,380 | 753 | 2,133 | 1,282 | 695 | 1,977 | 434 | 229 | 663 | 370 | 197 | 567 | 558 | 323 | 881 | 5,577 | 3,581 | 9,158 | 9,601 | 5,778 | 15,379 |
| 7. | Jos | 899 | 382 | 1,281 | 1,564 | 1,225 | 2,789 | 572 | 1,409 | 1,981 | 905 | 231 | 1,136 | 5,282 | 1,680 | 6,962 | 1,063 | 440 | 1,503 | 10,285 | 5,367 | 15,652 |
| 8. | Calabar | 283 | 95 | 378 | 1,514 | 816 | 2,330 | 31 | 14 | 45 | 29 | 10 | 39 | 323 | 73 | 396 | 3,661 | 1,550 | 5,211 | 5,841 | 2,558 | 8,399 |
| 9. | Kano | 131 | 17 | 148 | 98 | 7 | 105 | 4,785 | 1,937 | 6,722 | 695 | 116 | 811 | 816 | 189 | 1,005 | 182 | 7 | 189 | 6,707 | 2,273 | 8,980 |
| 10. | Maiduguri | 323 | 104 | 427 | 281 | 146 | 427 | 434 | 88 | 522 | 4,460 | 1,424 | 5,884 | 519 | 205 | 724 | 222 | 112 | 334 | 6,239 | 2,079 | 8,318 |
| 11. | Sokoto | 180 | 61 | 241 | 93 | 62 | 155 | 2,539 | 392 | 2,931 | 3,019 | 17 | 3,036 | 1,062 | 149 | 1,211 | 105 | 41 | 146 | 6,998 | 722 | 7,720 |
| 12. | Ilorin | 3,629 | 1,099 | 4,728 | 129 | 87 | 216 | 27 | 2 | 29 | 122 | 32 | 154 | 3,118 | 998 | 4,116 | 439 | 143 | 582 | 7,464 | 2,361 | 9,825 |
| 13. | Port Harcourt | 366 | 256 | 622 | 1,259 | 1,332 | 2,591 | 0 | 0 | 0 | 4 | 3 | 7 | 192 | 180 | 372 | 4,007 | 3,129 | 7,136 | 5,828 | 4,900 | 10,729 |
| 14. | Bauchi | 230 | 80 | 310 | 215 | 66 | 281 | 305 | 60 | 365 | 467 | 120 | 587 | 515 | 124 | 639 | 208 | 63 | 271 | 1,940 | 513 | 2,453 |
| 15. | Makurdi | 147 | 35 | 182 | 123 | 54 | 177 | 16 | 1 | 17 | 20 | 1 | 21 | 723 | 89 | 812 | 139 | 33 | 172 | 1,168 | 213 | 1,381 |
| 16. | Oweri | 94 | 12 | 106 | 1,633 | 229 | 1,862 | 3 | 0 | 3 | 1 | 0 | 1 | 39 | 0 | 39 | 379 | 7 | 386 | 2,149 | 248 | 2,397 |
| 17. | Yola | 128 | 36 | 164 | 128 | 63 | 191 | 242 | 23 | 265 | 1,238 | 259 | 1,497 | 189 | 57 | 246 | 137 | 44 | 181 | 2,062 | 482 | 2,544 |
| 18. | Akure | 1,454 | 242 | 1,696 | 64 | 17 | 81 | 2 | 1 | 3 | 5 | 0 | 5 | 52 | 6 | 58 | 227 | 17 | 244 | 1,804 | 283 | 2,087 |
| 19. | Abeokuta | 906 | 273 | 1,179 | 56 | 16 | 72 | 1 | 0 | 1 | 10 | 1 | 11 | 50 | 11 | 61 | 109 | 32 | 141 | 1,132 | 333 | 1,465 |
| 20. | Minna | 234 | 53 | 287 | 84 | 25 | 109 | 91 | 12 | 103 | 25 | 4 | 29 | 716 | 113 | 829 | 156 | 35 | 191 | 1,306 | 242 | 1,548 |
| 21. | Abuja | 38 | 25 | 63 | 35 | 37 | 72 | 56 | 46 | 102 | 39 | 22 | 61 | 125 | 66 | 191 | 41 | 52 | 93 | 334 | 248 | 582 |
| 22. | Uyo | 64 | 20 | 84 | 442 | 345 | 787 | 1 | 0 | 1 | 3 | 1 | 4 | 15 | 9 | 24 | 4,030 | 2,201 | 6,231 | 4,555 | 2,576 | 7,131 |
| | Total Per Zone | 32,034 | 10,794 | 42,828 | 21,261 | 11,865 | 33,126 | 12,579 | 4,807 | 17,386 | 13,106 | 2,790 | 15,896 | 20,306 | 5,718 | 26,024 | 27,343 | 13,900 | 41,243 | 126,629 | 49,874 | 176,503 |

Source: *National Universities Commission Statistical Digest 1988-1992*, Abuja: National Universities Commission, 1992

## Table 4.21: Enrolment into Federal Universities by Region, Academic Years 1980/81-1991/92

| Region Enrolment | 1980/81 | % | 1981/82 | % | 1982/83 | % | 1983/84 | % | 1984/85 | % | 1985/86 | % | 1986/87 | % | 1988/89 | % | 1989/90 | % | 1990/91 | % | 1991/92 | % |
|---|---|---|---|---|---|---|---|---|---|---|---|---|---|---|---|---|---|---|---|---|---|---|
| North | 18135 | 269 | 22551 | 276 | 25570 | 284 | 29691 | 302 | 33310 | 310 | 33709 | 309 | 36236 | 315 | 38173 | 293 | 42682 | 320 | 46063 | 311 | 59306 | 336 |
| South | 49283 | 731 | 59216 | 724 | 64496 | 716 | 68676 | 698 | 73971 | 690 | 75414 | 691 | 78863 | 685 | 92157 | 707 | 90711 | 680 | 102260 | 689 | 117197 | 664 |
| Total | 67,418 | 100 | 81,767 | 100 | 90,066 | 100 | 98,367 | 100 | 107,281 | 100 | 109,123 | 100 | 115,159 | 100 | 130,330 | 100 | 133,393 | 100 | 148,343 | 100 | 176,503 | 100 |

## Table 4.22a: Zonal Share of Federal Expenditure on Education from 1981-1992 Derived from the Summation of per Student (capita) Shares (₦)*

| Academic Year | Zone 1 | Zone 2 | Zone 3 | Zone 4 | Zone 5 | Zone 6 | Total |
|---|---|---|---|---|---|---|---|
| 1980/81 | 87,056,456.34 | 72,915,917.16 | 22,141,472.94 | 20,085,677.46 | 41,740,982.55 | 68,216,294.61 | 312,156,801.06 |
| 1981/82 | 95,278,466.22 | 72,083,244.48 | 25,210,812.02 | 19,259,642.30 | 45,358,748.06 | 68,518,119.38 | 325,709,032.46 |
| 1982/83 | 104,437,699.92 | 81,175,134.96 | 28,570,201.20 | 23,937,195.60 | 51,410,106.00 | 77,314,296.96 | 366,844,634.64 |
| 1983/84 | 123,380,317.50 | 87,419,962.50 | 37,131,177.50 | 32,195,442.50 | 59,903,457.50 | 88,112,010.00 | 428,142,367.50 |
| 1984/85 | 120,320,821.04 | 85,719,397.12 | 38,072,179.04 | 31,838,184.00 | 61,019,255.36 | 84,713,153.28 | 421,682,989.84 |
| 1985/86 | 112,227,512.10 | 80,030,603.62 | 35,985,401.98 | 28,225,157.62 | 54,586,024.02 | 73,514,394.80 | 384,569,094.14 |
| 1986/87 | 90,719,281.60 | 58,235,502.40 | 26,915,352.00 | 24,655,028.80 | 41,870,041.60 | 54,070,123.20 | 296,465,329.60 |
| 1987/88 | – | – | – | – | – | – | – |
| 1988/89 | 172,039,336.90 | 125,198,861.04 | 48,755,240.06 | 40,673,153.96 | 80,553,684.60 | 113,131,393.64 | 580,351,670.20 |
| 1989/90 | 164,389,648.73 | 117,123,171.49 | 50,696,000.97 | 46,566,837.23 | 85,939,829.94 | 107,843,283.79 | 572,558,772.15 |
| 1990/91 | 159,942,422.34 | 121,560,688.17 | 51,818,017.68 | 49,800,310.38 | 88,140,866.85 | 139,580,049.69 | 610,842,355.11 |
| 1991/92 | 494,720,789.52 | 382,649,688.84 | 200,831,597.24 | 183,620,100.64 | 300,612,072.16 | 476,411,915.62 | 2,038,846,164.02 |
| Total | 1,724,512,752.21 | 1,284,112,171.78 | 566,127,450.63 | 500,856,730.49 | 911,135,068.64 | 1,351,425,034.97 | 6,338,169,210.72 |

* Per capita cost of federal expenditure is calculated by dividing the total federal expenditure on education by the total number of students in federal universities per year.

It is relevant at this juncture to note the phenomenon of switching state of origin among southerners in seeking explanations for the increase in northern enrolment figures. Intent on beating the quota principle, which is applied in favour of northern candidates but denying them admission with better qualifications as claimants of states of origin in the south, 'smart' southern folks have adopted northern states of origin to gain admission into universities located in the south. Some have confidentially admitted it to perceptive colleagues at the University of Ibadan, situated in the South-West of Nigeria when confronted. Shared Muslim names and other cultural symbols have made such 'impersonations' possible. This being the case, it must mean that 'southerners' form part of the northern enrolment figures.

The gaps in enrolments between zones and regions by themselves indicate the differentials in the zonal or regional share of federal expenditure on university education. These differentials become more evident when relating the cost of providing university education to the total student enrolment by zone and region. Thus, as Table 22a shows, the South-West consistently took the largest share of federal expenditure on education from the 1980/81 session up to the 1991/92 session. It was followed by the South-East until the 1983/84 session when the South-South beat it marginally to third position. The South-East returned to the second largest position the following year and maintained this until 1991 when the South-South again moved and remained in second position in the 1991/92 academic year.

The South-West's share from the table is triple that of the North-East's, much more so of the North-West's and almost double the North-Central's during the period. The South-West's share is more than the North-East's and the North-West's combined and almost the sum of the whole north's, that is, including the remaining North-Central's share. The South-East's and South-South's separate share is double that of the North-East's and North-West's and of course, more than the North-Central's share. Table 22b makes the south's share, which is more than double the north's, even more obvious. When the incidence of claiming a northern state of origin by southerners seeking to exploit the preferential admission criterion for northern candidates is factored in, the north's share of federal expenditure on education is further reduced.

### Table 4.22b: The North-South Share of Federal Expenditure on Education in 1981-1992 Derived from the Summation of Per Student (capita) share

| Zone | Share (₦) | % |
|------|-----------|---|
| North | 1,978,119,251.76 | 31.2 |
| South | 4,360,049,958.96 | 68.8 |
| Total | 6,338,169,210.72 | 100 |

Source: Computed from NUC Annual Reports, Abuja.

There is also the fact that northern zones are acutely under-subscribed in science courses, which cost the government more money. Take for example their enrolment share between 1980 and 1986 in medicine, the most expensive course to run. As tables 22a and 22b show, the north's share averaged only 15.85 per cent. Thus, the entire north's enrolment of 7,502 was less than the smallest of the southern zonal enrolment, that is, 11,721 of Zone 6. In that case, the north's acute under-subscription in science courses leaves it with an even smaller real share of federal expenditure on education than the general distribution of zonal and regional shares portray. If the basis of comparison of benefits and losses is shifted from physically bounded identities in line with trans-physical boundaries of ethnic identities when groups are in competition for resources at the national level, the gaps become wider.[2]

The Yoruba who are predominant in the South-West and are present in very significant numbers in the states of Kwara and Kogi, which take the lion's share of the North-Central's enrolment of in north and therefore the largest share of the north's federal expenditure on education, are much bigger gainers than portrayed by the statistics presented above.

### Table 4.23a: Enrolment into Federal Universities for Medicine by Zone for the Academic Sessions 1980/81–1985/86

| Academic year | Zone 1 | Zone 2 | Zone 3 | Zone 4 | Zone 5 | Zone 6 |
|---|---|---|---|---|---|---|
| 1980/81 | 1,918 | 1,710 | 120 | 131 | 713 | 1,664 |
| 1981/82 | 2,492 | 1,765 | 152 | 174 | 786 | 1,851 |
| 1982/83 | 2,574 | 2,063 | 174 | 239 | 835 | 2,029 |
| 1983/84 | 2,896 | 2,048 | 206 | 301 | 878 | 2,089 |
| 1984/85 | 2,994 | 2,078 | 242 | 369 | 601 | 1,996 |
| 1985/86 | 3,222 | 2,196 | 237 | 408 | 936 | 2,092 |
| Total | 16,096 | 11,860 | 1,131 | 1,622 | 4,749 | 11,721 |

Source: Computed from NUC Annual Reports, Abuja.

### Table 4.23b: Enrolment into Federal Universities for Medicine by Region, for the Academic Sessions 1980/81-1985/86

| Region | 1980/81 Enrol-ment | % | 1981/82 % | 1982/83 % | 1983/84 % | 1984/85 % | 1985/86 % |
|---|---|---|---|---|---|---|---|
| North | 964 | 15.4 | 1,112 15.4 | 1,248 15.8 | 1,385 16.5 | 1,212 14.6 | 1,581 17.4 |
| South | 5,292 | 84.6 | 6,108 84.6 | 6,666 84.2 | 7,033 83.5 | 7,068 85.4 | 7,510 82.6 |
| Total | 6,256 | 100 | 7,220 100 | 7,914 100 | 8,418 100 | 8,280 100 | 9,091 100 |

Source: Computed from NUC Annual Reports, Abuja.

If the pattern of enrolment into federal universities that produced this skewed southern share of federal expenditure on universities is the same to date, as there is strong reason to b lieve, it is safe to conclude that the South has consistently taken more than half of the federal government's expenditure on education since 1980. If, furthermore, northern enrolment patterns are worse than those used to reach the above conclusions, the computation of the regional distribution of the share of federal expenditure will reveal a wider gap between the North and South.

## Conclusion

The federal military government apparently intended to use the sole responsibility for university education that it arrogated to itself in 1977 to redistribute access in favour of the northern region, which was well known to be behind the southern region in educational development. However from the regional distribution of enrolments into federal universities and consequent upon it, regional shares of federal expenditure on university education, national resources are thereby inadvertently being used to enhance university education in the educationally advanced southern region. That being the case, the more or longer that the federal government is involved in the running of universities, the more or longer will the south take the lion's share of what it puts in. Similarly, if there is no reason to believe that the enrolment patterns are different in federal secondary schools, colleges of education and polytechnics, the conclusions made above then have multiple significances. It follows that the attempt to use JAMB to redress the imbalance between the south and north in enrolment into federal universities through admission quotas has achieved only very modest results. As such, other more result-oriented strategies are recommended.

## Notes

1.  For example, the University of Ibadan, the Nigerian premier University's 2004/2005 academic session ends on 10 March 2006. See University of Ibadan Official Bulletin 2 June 2005.
2.  The Kwara and Kogi Yorubas have been seen more as part of the South-West than the North, which they belong to in terms of geographic location, because of their ethnic configuration. For example, the Senate of Nigeria in 2002 refused to endorse President Olusegun Obasanjo's proposal to appoint a Yoruba from Kogi State (North-Central), Mr. J.O. Ajiboye, on the grounds that his appointment would contravene the provision of Section 14(3) of the Constitution, which states that:

    The composition of the Government of the Federation or any of its agencies and the conduct of its affairs shall be carried out in such a manner as to reflect the federal character of Nigeria and the need to promote national unity, and also to command national loyalty, thereby ensuring that there shall be no predominance of persons from a few States or from a few ethnic or other sectional groups in that Government or in any of its agencies.

## References

Abdulkadir I. A., 'Introduction', in A.U. Kadiri ed., 1987, *25 Years of Centralizing University Education in Nigeria*, Lagos: NUC, pp. 1-4.

Adam, Mahdi, 'Withdrawal of Subsidies in the Education System in Nigeria: How Feasible and How Advisable' in Mahdi Adamu ed., 1986, *University Education: Its Standard and Relevance to the Nigerian Community – Proceedings of a Joint Seminar Organized by the CVC of Nigerian Universities and the NUC*, held at Usman Danfodio University, 17-19 March, Sokoto.

Akangbou, S. D., 1980, 'The Preliminary Analysis of Recurrent Unit Cost of Higher Education in Nigeria: The Case of the University of Ibadan,' *The Nigerian Journal of Economic and Social Studies*, Vol. 22, No.3, pp. 395-412.

Aminu, J., 'Traffic Warden at Ribadu Road' in A.U. Kadiri ed., 1987, *25 Years of Centralizing University Education in Nigeria*, Lagos: NUC, pp. 8-49.

Angulu, M., 'JAMB – Were the Critics Right?', in A.U. Kadiri ed., 1987, *25 Years of Centralizing University Education in Nigeria*, Lagos: NUC, pp.109-113.

Briggs, B., 1980, 'Federal Character and Higher Education in Nigeria', *Bulletin of the National Universities Commission*, Lagos, July-September, Vol. 2, No.2, 47-74.

National Universities Commission Secretariat, 'Historical Evolution of the National Universities Commission (the Secretariat and the Board) 1962-1988, A. U. Kadiri ed., 1987, *25 Years of Centralizing University Education in Nigeria*, Lagos: NUC.

Fafunwa, A. B., 1994, *History of Education in Nigeria, New Edition*, Ibadan: NPS Educational Publishers Ltd.

Ike, V. C., 'A Critique of Admission and Pedagogical Policies and Practices in the Nigerian University', in Mahdi Adamu ed., 1986, *University Education: Its Standard and Relevance to the Nigerian Community – Proceedings of a Joint Seminar Organized by the CVC of Nigerian Universities and the NUC*, held at Usman Danfodio University, 17-19 March, Sokoto.

Kadiri, A. U., ed., 1975, *25 Years of Centralizing University Education in Nigeria*, Lagos: NUC, pp.114-125.

Mbanefoh, G. F., 1980, 'Sharing the Costs and Benefits of University Education in Nigeria: A Suggested Approach', *The Nigerian Journal of Economic and Social Studies*, Vol. 22, No.1, pp.67-83.

Oladapo, I. O., 'The Emergence of State and Private Universities', in A.U. Kadiri ed, 1975, *25 Years of Centralizing University Education in Nigeria*, Lagos: NUC, pp.59-73.

Salim, B. A., 2003, ' Problems of Assessment and Selection into Tertiary Institutions in Nigeria', Paper presented at the 21st Annual Conference of AEAA held at Cape Town, South Africa from 25-29 August 2003.

Tamuno, T. N., 'Management of the Universities in Nigeria: A Look at the Past, the Present and the Future', NUC, 1987, *Resource Management in the University System, Proceedings of the NUC-CVC-BC International Seminar*, ABU, Zaria, 9-10 November pp.15-29.

Ukwu, I. U., 'Federal Financing of Projects for National Development and integration', in Ukwu, I. Ukwu ed., 1987, *Federal Character and National Integration in Nigeria*, Kuru, Jos: National Institute for Policy and Strategic Studies, pp.113-129.

Yoloye, E. A., 1989, 'Federal Character and Institutions of Higher Learning', in P. P. Ekeh & E. E. Osaghae, *Federal Character and Federalism in Nigeria*, Ibadan: Heinemann Educational Books Ltd.

Young, M. C., 1981, 'The African University: Universalism, Development, and Ethnicity', *Comparative Education Review*, Vol. 25, No. 2. pp. 145-163.

# 5

## Federal Public Service as a Cake to be Shared

### The Development of the Public Service

The term 'public service' is used to embrace the civil service, parastatals and other extra ministerial government agencies. It is a colonial creation whose shape and structure was influenced by the colonial system of rule. In other words, the development of the public service closely followed Nigeria's constitutional development under colonial rule. Prior to colonial rule, disparate and largely decentralized systems of administration existed in different parts of Nigeria. While the north operated a highly centralized and authoritarian system of administration known as the Emirate system, which later provided the basis for the Indirect Rule system of administration, the Yoruba (west) and Bini (mid-west) practiced a somewhat less autocratic and less centralized monarchical system of administration. On the other hand, various groups in the coastal parts of the east practised a semi-monarchical system of administration while the Igbo in the southeast practised highly decentralized republican systems based on the principles of equality and individualism. Such traditional systems of administration were reconstituted into Native Administrations under the Indirect Rule System with chiefs and all those who served under them forming the lower stratum of the public service. Of course, the European administrators formed the top stratum.

Even with the centralist thrust of colonial rule, public administration (or to be specific, the civil service) had to be modelled after the diversity of Nigeria. The influence of cultural and other differences on the development of the civil service is best captured by the concept of regionalism. This concept sprang from two views. The first concerned the cultivation of the then three administrative regions into three self-governing countries. The second considered the reconstitution of the Native Authorities into local governments as channels of political representation in the parliament and executive council both of which were centralized. The colonial regime adopted regionalization as an administrative structure to satisfy partially the desire to give the north an opportunity to grow politically and economically at its pace and to avoid, for the colonial regime, the uncontrolled presence of educated elite in the central government. In the latter case, regionalization was an instrument of diffusion and, overall, a compromise between separatists and strong federalists (Coleman 1958).

However, the public service remained one even with the tripartite regional administrative structure put in place by the Richards Constitution of 1946. The only concrete expression of regionalization and semblance of a federal structure was the House of Assembly existing in each region as an intermediate organization between the Native Authorities and the colonial government whose functions were no more than deliberative and advisory (Gboyega 2003). Thus, up to 1954, public service was unitary and under the control of the governor. The editor of *Gaskiya Ta Fi Kwabo*, a northern based newspaper describes the north's share of public service posts in 1950 during this unitary era of the civil service thus:

> ...There are Europeans but, undoubtedly, it is the Southerner who has the power in the North. They have control of the railway stations; of the Post Offices; of Government Hospitals; of the canteens; the majority employed in the Kaduna Secretariat and in the Public Works Department are all Southerners; in all the different departments of Government it is the Southerner who has the power... (quoted in Coleman 1958:362).

This situation led to anti-southern sentiments among northern elites and subsequently to the 'northernization' policy in which the north sought to reduce and/or restrict southerners' influx into its civil service after the 1954 Constitution regionalized the civil service.

This policy meant that northern political leaders showed a preference for non-Nigerians to southerners in filling vacancies in the northern civil service because according to their observation, 'Nigerian officers of non-Northern origin tend to settle in the North with their families and relations' (quoted in Onajide 1979:28). Their explanation of the preference for expatriates to southern Nigerians was that the 'Southern settler was in the habit of doing certain undesirable things, like taking a lease of land and exploiting the service of Northern peasants in the cultivation of it, and secondly, that when a Southerner became a foreman the junior positions in the works very soon changed hands from Northern holders to his brothers and cousins brought over from the south' (quoted in Onajide 1979:28). Granted that these allegations are true and from the viewpoint of national integration as Mr. Simeon Adebo, a highly respected Nigerian civil servant from the Yoruba West aptly observed, 'the way to combat them is not by the denial of employment to prevent the Southerner from settling in the North but by appropriate byelaws, rules or regulations, directly to attack the abuses aimed at' (quoted in Onajide 1979:29). However, this sound analysis notwithstanding, rejection of southerners continued under the northernization policy.

With the regionalization of the civil service, each of the three regions and the federal government had a Public Service Commission while the local government had the Local Government Service Boards. In that set-up, the Governor or Governor-General made appointments into the civil service on the recommendation of the Commission (Sklar 1963). During these early years of regionalization, also known as the de-colonizing years of the 1950s, the civil service was faced with two antithetical orientations: either be a service that can rise above sectional demands or be one that reflects in numbers the balance between the groups that are behind the demands (Joseph 1991). The attraction to the latter was strong because of the drive for 'Nigerianization'. By 1960, the year of political independence, about 60 per cent of senior posts were occupied by Nigerians. The majority of expatriates who occupied the remaining 40 per cent did so on 'short-term contract service' (Sklar 1963:497).

The regional share of the federal civil service even though skewed in favour of one (the southern) part of the country may have been tolerated because the regions were the centre of the drive for rapid change and development and as such, the repository of effective decision-making power. Even at that, the centre was attractive in so far as its civil service had posts to be filled. Hence, the National Council of Nigerian Citizens (NCNC) joined the Northern Peoples Congress (NPC) rather than the Action Group (AG) in a coalition government in 1959 in the calculation that its people in the eastern region would have a better chance in the competition for federal jobs because NPC had less qualified people than the NCNC (Dudley 1982; Gboyega 1997; Ikime 2002). Indeed, the NCNC remained in alliance in spite of its disenchantment with the NPC over the 1964 federal elections by participating in the NPC-led government after the elections (Schwarz 1968). Before long, a faction of AG was weary of being in the opposition because as Schwarz (1968:130) put it, 'lacking federal power meant ... fewer scholarships, factories, jobs, loans and amenities for one's region'. Thus, the Unification Decree of May 1966 that aimed at unifying all civil services in a fell swoop overstretched the forbearance of the north toward the south's disproportionate share of federal civil service posts. It swiftly reacted through organized massacres targeted mainly at the Igbo in their midst. In response, the Igbo-led government of the Eastern Region declared secession in 1967. The determination of the northern-led federal government under General Yakubu Gowon to quell the secession led inexorably to the thirty-month civil war of 1967-70.

The federal civil service began to have a real taste of power after independence especially under the military, which many scholars had accurately predicted would tend to lead to an expanded role of state bureaucracy after military seizure of power (Joseph 1991). Increasingly, the civil service at the centre became the 'national cake' out of which ethno-regional groups sought to have as large a share as possible (cited in Joseph 1991). This means that civil service employment is perceived in Nigeria first as a means of sharing and then, if at all, as a means of getting a job done. Individuals who as private proprietors recruit not on the basis of state or ethnic origin but on qualification or competence are as a result staunch advocates of ethnic principle for recruitment into public service. Hence, 'standards of recruitment, measurement of performance and advancement within the federal civil service have been varied in the pursuit of ...federal balance of ethnic groups and states' over the years (Asiodu 1979:92). The Udoji Public Services Review Commission Report of 1974 intensified this perception of the federal civil service as a cake to be shared by downgrading 'state civil services to a second order of importance,' notably in remuneration (Olugbemi 1979:102).

## Recruitment Procedures

The 1999 Constitution endows the Federal Civil Service Commission in the Third Schedule Part 1 (D) with the power
  (a) to appoint persons to offices in the Federal civil service, and
  (b) to dismiss and exercise disciplinary control over persons holding such offices.
However, Section 170 of the constitution provides that the commission can with the approval of the President, 'delegate any of the powers conferred upon it by the Constitution to any of its members or to any officer in the civil service of the Federation.' It is along this line that each ministry or extra-ministerial department can fill posts of grade levels 01-06 with people who have the required qualifications from the state in which the establishment is situated in a manner that reflects the ethno-administrative diversity of the state. Appointments into grade levels 07-10 posts are made on the authority of the Federal Civil Service Commission. Grade levels 12-17 posts are to be filled after advertisement in consultation with the Head of Service of the Federation. Permanent Secretaries and Heads of Extra-Ministerial Departments can promote officers to posts within their power of appointment (Federal Republic of Nigeria 2000). Concern for equity in the sharing of all resources and benefits under the control of the government led to the insertion of a principle of sharing, known as the Federal Character Principle in the 1979 Constitution. Successive constitutions – the never-implemented 1989 constitution now superseded by the 1999 Constitution – contain this provision.

Perhaps out of suspicion that the federal character principle was not being implemented to the letter, the 1994 constitutional conference recommended the establishment of the Federal Character Commission in the 1995 draft constitution. The General Sani Abacha Administration, which immediately convened the conference, adopted this recommendation. The administration was itself suspect for this action given that other recommendations in the draft constitution such as rotational presidency, power-sharing, and greater emphasis on the derivation principle in revenue allocation, which almost half of Nigeria felt were even more urgent, received no attention. The adoption of the recommendation of the Commission out of equally, if not more, pressing demands was thus a repeat of the self-serving selective implementation of recommendations by the General Ibrahim Babangida Administration, which accepted the recommendation for the postponement of the handover date from 1990 to 1992 while rejecting the recommendation of socialist ideology by the Political Bureau (Political Bureau 1987). The suspicion of bad faith in the adoption of the recommendation also issues from the imbalances that, even some northerners acknowledged, existed between the north and south in favour of the former in the distribution of headships of major state organs and establishments under General Abacha (Isumonah 2003). The impure motive of the administration could not have been more self-betraying than the fact that the commission was itself guilty of disregard for Nigeria's ethnic diversity with its composition by 1998 when it collapsed under Abacha's demise – the Chair, Secretary, eight out of the twelve management staff of the commission and ninety per cent of the rank and file staff being from the north (Nyiam 1999).

Nevertheless, the commission was entrenched in the 1999 Constitution by his successor, General Abdulsalami Abubakar, and empowered to enforce the federal character principle in all federal establishments with regards to the posts 'of the Permanent Secretaries, Directors-General in Extra-Ministerial Departments and Parastatals, Directors in Ministries and Extra-Ministerial Departments, senior military officers, senior diplomatic posts and managerial cadres in the Federal and State parastatals, bodies, agencies and institutions' (Third Schedule Part 1 C, 1999 Constitution). Consequently, the commission has adopted a formula, which states that 'at the national level the indigenes of a state shall constitute not less than 2.5 per cent and not more than 3 per cent; and the indigenes of a zone shall constitute not less than 15 per cent and not more than 18 per cent' (Federal Character Commission, *This Day*, Lagos, 4 October 1999).

**Table 5.1: Federal Civil Service 1996 Manpower Statistics Distribution of 63,867 Staff on Grade Level 08 and Above**

| Zone | No. | % | Zone | No. | % |
|---|---|---|---|---|---|
| **South West** | 17,767 | 27.8 | **South-South** | 13,007 | 20.4 |
| Ogun | 5,023 | 7.9 | Delta | 3,969 | 6.2 |
| Ondo/Ekiti | 4,932 | 7.7 | Edo | 3,436 | 5.4 |
| Oyo | 3,073 | 4.8 | Akwa Ibom | 2,319 | 3.6 |
| Osun | 2,393 | 3.7 | River/Bayelsa | 1,783 | 2.8 |
| Lagos | 2,346 | 3.7 | Cross River | 1,497 | 2.3 |

| Zone | No. | % | Zone | No. | % |
|---|---|---|---|---|---|
| **South East** | 11,842 | 18.5 | **North Central** | 10,578 | 16.6 |
| Imo | 4,794 | 7.5 | Kogi | 2,462 | 3.9 |
| Anambra | 3,942 | 6.2 | Kwara | 2,203 | 3.4 |
| Abia/Ebonyi | 1,948 | 3.1 | Plateau/Nasarawa | 2,202 | 3.4 |
| Enugu/Ebonyi | 1,158 | 1.8 | Benue | 1,847 | 2.9 |
| Niger | 1,596 | 2.5 | | | |
| FCT | 268 | 0.4 | | | |

| Zone | No. | % | Zone | No. | % |
|---|---|---|---|---|---|
| **North West** | 5,850 | 9.2 | **North East** | 4,794 | 7.5 |
| Kaduna | 1,836 | 2.9 | Bauchi/Gombe | 1,356 | 2.1 |
| Kano | 1,245 | 1.9 | Adamawa | 1,184 | 1.9 |
| Katsina | 1,147 | 1.8 | Borno | 1,130 | 1.8 |
| Sokoto/Zamfara | 631 | 1.0 | Taraba | 626 | 1.0 |
| Kebbi | 624 | 1.0 | Yobe | 498 | 0.8 |
| Jigawa | 367 | 0.6 | | | |

Source: Federal Character Commission Press Release, *ThisDay*, Lagos, 4 October, 1999

### Table 5.2: Federal Civil Service 1996 Manpower Statistics Distribution of 2,776 Staff on Grade Level 15 and Above

| Zone | No. | % | Zone | No. | % |
|------|-----|---|------|-----|---|
| **South West** | 820 | 29.5 | **South South** | 429 | 15.5 |
| Ogun | 254 | 9.1 | Edo | 170 | 6.1 |
| Ondo/Ekiti | 214 | 7.7 | Delta | 140 | 5.0 |
| Oyo | 138 | 5.0 | Akwa-Ibom | 51 | 1.8 |
| Osun | 122 | 4.4 | Cross River | 44 | 1.6 |
| Lagos | 92 | 3.3 | Rivers/Bayelsa | 24 | 0.9 |
| **Zone** | **No.** | **%** | **Zone** | **No.** | **%** |
| **South East** | 437 | 15.7 | **North Central** | 456 | 16.4 |
| Anambra | 188 | 6.8 | Kwara | 102 | 3.7 |
| Imo | 141 | 5.1 | Kogi | 94 | 3.4 |
| Abia/Ebonyi | 70 | 2.5 | Niger | 87 | 3.1 |
| Enugu/Ebonyi | 38 | 1.4 | Plateau/Nasarawa | 86 | 3.1 |
| | | | Benue | 78 | 2.8 |
| | | | FCT | 9 | 0.3 |
| **Zone** | **No.** | **%** | **Zone** | **No.** | **%** |
| **North West** | 339 | 12.2 | **North East** | 291 | 10.5 |
| Kaduna | 92 | 3.3 | Adamawa | 98 | 3.5 |
| Kano | 74 | 2.7 | Bauchi/Gombe | 71 | 2.6 |
| Katsina | 66 | 2.4 | Borno | 64 | 2.3 |
| Jigawa | 47 | 1.7 | Taraba | 30 | 1.1 |
| Sokoto/Zamfara | 37 | 1.3 | Yobe | 28 | 1.0 |
| Kebbi | 23 | 0.8 | | | |

Source: Federal Character Commission Press Release, *ThisDay*, Lagos, 4 October, 1999

### Table 5.3: 122 Federal Statutory and State-owned Companies - 1996 Manpower Consolidated Statistics - Distribution of 60,887 Staff on Grade Level 08 and Above

| Zone | No. | % | Zone | No. | % |
|------|-----|---|------|-----|---|
| **South West** | 18,589 | 30.5 | **South-South** | 13,242 | 21.7 |
| Ogun | 5,729 | 9.4 | Delta | 5,180 | 8.5 |
| Ondo/Ekiti | 4,602 | 7.6 | Edo | 3,799 | 6.2 |
| Oyo | 3,902 | 6.4 | Akwa Ibom | 2,026 | 3.3 |
| Osun | 3,001 | 4.9 | River/Bayelsa | 1,485 | 2.4 |
| Lagos | 1,355 | 2.2 | Cross River | 752 | 1.2 |
| **Zone** | **No.** | **%** | **Zone** | **No.** | **%** |
| **South East** | 13,076 | 21.5 | **North Central** | 7,833 | 12.9 |
| Imo | 4,678 | 7.7 | Kogi | 2,163 | 3.6 |
| Anambra | 3,375 | 5.5 | Kwara | 1,929 | 3.2 |
| Abia/Ebonyi | 2,840 | 4.7 | Plateau/Nasarawa | 1,299 | 2.1 |
| Enugu/Ebonyi | 2,183 | 3.6 | Benue | 1,263 | 2.1 |
| | | | Niger | 1,100 | 1.8 |
| | | | FCT | 79 | 0.1 |
| **Zone** | **No.** | **%** | **Zone** | **No.** | **%** |
| **North West** | 4,813 | 7.9 | **North East** | 3,301 | 5.4 |
| Kaduna | 1,954 | 3.2 | Bauchi/Gombe | 1,000 | 1.6 |
| Kano | 999 | 1.6 | Adamawa | 921 | 1.5 |
| Katsina | 643 | 1.1 | Borno | 803 | 1.3 |
| Sokoto/Zamfara | 442 | 0.7 | Taraba | 329 | 0.5 |
| Kebbi | 421 | 0.7 | Yobe | 248 | 0.4 |
| Jigawa | 354 | 0.6 | | | |

Source: Federal Character Commission Press Release, *ThisDay*, Lagos, 4 October, 1999

## Table 5.4: 122 Federal Statutory and State-owned Companies 1996 Manpower Consolidated Statistics Distribution of 1,823 Staff on Grade Level 15 and Above

| Zone | No. | % | Zone | No. | % |
|---|---|---|---|---|---|
| South West | 513 | 28.1 | South South | 312 | 17.1 |
| Ogun | 157 | 8.6 | Edo | 108 | 5.9 |
| Ondo/Ekiti | 108 | 5.9 | Delta | 98 | 5.4 |
| Osun | 102 | 5.6 | Akwa-Ibom | 44 | 2.4 |
| Oyo | 78 | 4.3 | Cross River | 32 | 1.8 |
| Lagos | 68 | 3.7 | Rivers/Bayelsa | 30 | 1.6 |

| Zone | No. | % | Zone | No. | % |
|---|---|---|---|---|---|
| South East | 339 | 18.6 | North Central | 271 | 14.9 |
| Anambra | 161 | 8.8 | Kwara | 79 | 4.3 |
| Imo | 87 | 4.8 | Kogi | 72 | 3.9 |
| Abia/Ebonyi | 58 | 3.2 | Niger | 40 | 2.2 |
| Enugu/Ebonyi | 33 | 1.8 | Plateau/Nasarawa | 37 | 2.0 |
| | | | Benue | 36 | 2.0 |
| | | | FCT | 7 | 0.4 |

| Zone | No. | % | Zone | No. | % |
|---|---|---|---|---|---|
| North West | 202 | 11.1 | North East | 181 | 9.9 |
| Kaduna | 71 | 3.9 | Adamawa | 54 | 3.0 |
| Kano | 42 | 2.3 | Bauchi/Gombe | 52 | 2.9 |
| Katsina | 31 | 1.7 | Borno | 52 | 2.9 |
| Jigawa | 22 | 1.2 | Taraba | 12 | 0.7 |
| Sokoto/Zamfara | 20 | 1.1 | Yobe | 11 | 0.6 |
| Kebbi | 16 | 0.9 | | | |

Source: Federal Character Commission Press Release, *ThisDay*, Lagos, 4 October, 1999

The total number of federal employees in 1996 was 481,794. Out of this, 327,221 were in the civil service while 154,573 were in extra-ministerial agencies and state-owned enterprises. According to a survey of the Federal Ministry of Finance, Abuja, in the year 2000, the total number was reduced in 1999 to 238,372 against an established position of 259,753. According to the Federal Ministry of Finance, Abuja (2000:43), '33 per cent of institutions surveyed admitted that their organizations were overstaffed'. This was even after the downsizing exercise of 1999. However, the survey reveals that the civil service is 'overstaffed at the lower levels and overworked at the higher levels' and that it lacked staff 'in critical areas such as economics, finance, policy analysis, general management and information technology' (p. 43).

## Table 5.5: Number of Staff by State of Origin

| State of Origin | Number | % |
|---|---|---|
| Abia | 5,275 | 3.83 |
| Adamawa | 2,148 | 1.56 |
| Akwa Ibom | 7,357 | 5.35 |
| Anambra | 4,379 | 3.18 |
| Bauchi | 1,675 | 1.22 |
| Bayelsa | 1,067 | 0.78 |
| Benue | 5,289 | 3.84 |
| Borno | 2,353 | 1.71 |
| Cros River | 3,748 | 2.72 |
| Delta | 7,674 | 5.58 |
| Ebonyi | 896 | 0.65 |
| Edo | 6,914 | 5.02 |
| Ekiti | 4,271 | 3.10 |
| Enugu | 3,641 | 2.65 |
| Fct | 601 | 0.44 |
| Gombe | 1,317 | 0.96 |
| Imo | 8,441 | 6.13 |
| Jigawa | 894 | 0.65 |
| Kaduna | 4,980 | 3.62 |
| Kano | 2,222 | 1.61 |
| Kastina | 1,979 | 1.44 |
| Kebbi | 1,175 | 0.85 |
| Kogi | 6,891 | 5.01 |
| Kwara | 3,795 | 2.76 |
| Lagos | 4,768 | 3.47 |
| Nasarawa | 1,731 | 1.26 |
| Niger | 2,821 | 2.05 |
| Ogun | 11,717 | 8.52 |
| Ondo | 5,922 | 4.30 |
| Osun | 5,738 | 4.17 |
| Other Countries | 64 | 0.05 |
| Oyo | 6,172 | 4.49 |
| Plateau | 3,373 | 2.45 |
| Rivers | 2,351 | 1.71 |
| Sokoto | 990 | 0.72 |
| Taraba | 1,445 | 1.05 |
| Yobe | 864 | 0.63 |
| Zamfara | 659 | 0.48 |
| Total for all Ministries | 137,598 | 100.00 |

Source: Report of the Computerization of the Records of Civil Servants in the Federal Republic Service, 2003.

## Table 5.6: Zonal Totals

| Zone | Number of Civil Servants | % |
|---|---|---|
| 1 South-West | 38,588 | 28.05 |
| 2 South-East | 22,632 | 16.44 |
| 3 North-West | 12,899 | 9.37 |
| 4 North-East | 9,802 | 7.13 |
| 5 North-Central | 24,501 | 17.81 |
| 6 South-South | 29,111 | 21.16 |
| Other Nationalities | 64 | 0.05 |
| Total | 137,597 | 100.0 |

Source: Report of the Computerization of the Records of Civil Servants in the Federal Republic
Service, 2003.

## Figure 5.1: Graph Showing Distribution by State

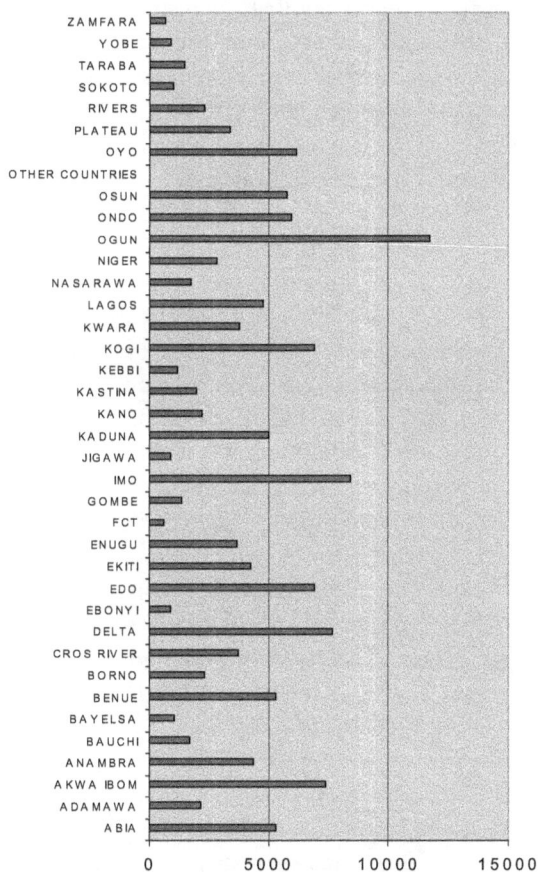

Source: Report of the Computerization of the Records of Civil Servants in the Federal Republic
Service, 2003.

The statistics presented and represented in the above tables and Figure 5.1 cover 24 Ministries, six Offices, three Commissions and four Units and exclude three ministries: Foreign Affairs, Health and Petroleum. The distribution by state of origin would remain significantly the same, in the opinion of the consultants who did the staff audit, were the statistics of the staff of these ministries included given that they have no more than 4,000 staff. On the basis of federal recurrent expenditure on the civil service, the preliminary inference from the statistics of the Federal Character Commission and Report of the Computerization of the Records of Civil Servants in the Federal Republic Service, 2003 above is that the zone that has the highest proportional mix of federal public service staff equally takes the lion's share of such federal resources. The actual zonal distribution of benefits is explicit in tables 5.7, 5.8 and 5.9.

Clearly, from Table 5.7, the South-West leads in terms of what zones derive from employment in the public service, specifically, salaries and emoluments. It is closely followed by the South-South and South-East respectively. The South-West's share is double the North-West's and is triple the North-East's. From Table 5.7, the South-South has the highest number of people in federal service public service but is beaten to the second position in its total share of federal recurrent expenditure by the South-West because of the latter's much higher representation in the top cadres. During the period covered by Table 5.7, the south had 192,929 (59 per cent) to the north's 133,946 (41 per cent) staff in federal ministries. The north's share in the highest senior cadres (GL 15-17) was 976 (37.5 per cent) to the south's 1,629 (62.5 per cent). Thus, the south took ₦10.7 billion (61.8 per cent) to the north's ₦6.6 billion (38.2 per cent). The zonal distribution of benefits follows the same patterns in Federal Statutory Bodies and State Owned Companies Zonal Consolidated Salary Statistics presented in Table 5.8 except that the north's overall share drops to 31.4 per cent (₦ 3.2 billion) from 38.2 per cent (₦6.6 billion) to the south's 68.6 per cent (₦ 7 billion). However the statistics in Tables 5.1 and 5.2 show that northern zones are relatively heavily represented in the highest posts (GL 16-17). The Northern figures are higher than the South-East's where they are not at par.

From Table 5.9, the differences in emoluments between the three highest senior cadres (Grade Levels 15-17) and three lowest junior cadres (Grade Levels 01-03) are between factors of 6 and 7. Similarly, the differences in emoluments between the three highest senior cadres (Grade Levels 15-17) and the highest junior cadre (Grade level 06) are between factors of 3.9 and 4.6. It should also be noted that the senior cadres enjoy all manner of unquantifiable perquisites of office in a progressive order. It is also at the senior cadres that allocation of resources, policy formulation and implementation takes place. It follows that the zones with greater representation in these management cadres, following the logic of ethnic competition for resources, are better placed to take more from federal resources via decisions on the distribution of capital projects and other mitigating expenditures of the federal government.

# Table 5.7: Salaries Earned by Zone in the Presidency, Federal Ministries and Extra-ministerial Department (GL 01-17) in Naira (₦)

| Grade Level (GL) | Zone 1 | | Zone 2 | | Zone 3 | | Zone 4 | | Zone 5 | | Zone 6 | | Total | |
|---|---|---|---|---|---|---|---|---|---|---|---|---|---|---|
| | No. of Staff | Salary | No. of Staff | Salary | No. of Staff | Salary | No. of Staff | Salary | No. of Staff | Salary | No. of Staff | Salary | No. of Staff | Salary |
| 01 | 2,986 | 84,294,780 | 1,209 | 34,130,070 | 1,948 | 54,992,040 | 1,028 | 29,020,440 | 2,381 | 67,215,630 | 2,649 | 74,781,270 | 12,201 | 344,434,230 |
| 02 | 2,860 | 86,194,680 | 1,539 | 46,291,968 | 1,952 | 58,829,376 | 1,213 | 36,557,394 | 3,322 | 100,118,436 | 3,007 | 90,624,966 | 13,890 | 418,616,820 |
| 03 | 12,180 | 389,881,800 | 4,801 | 153,680,010 | 10,730 | 343,467,300 | 4,911 | 157,201,110 | 14,528 | 465,041,280 | 13,694 | 438,344,940 | 60,844 | 1,947,616,440 |
| 04 | 9,901 | 356,851,842 | 7,964 | 287,038,488 | 6,143 | 221,406,006 | 5,543 | 199,780,806 | 12,169 | 438,595,098 | 13,189 | 475,357,938 | 54,909 | 1,979,030,178 |
| 05 | 10,282 | 420,184,212 | 8,335 | 340,618,110 | 5,227 | 213,606,582 | 4,703 | 192,192,798 | 12,182 | 497,829,612 | 14,140 | 577,845,240 | 54,869 | 2,242,276,554 |
| 06 | 6,715 | 324,186,770 | 4,233 | 204,360,774 | 2,645 | 127,695,310 | 2,848 | 137,495,744 | 4,515 | 217,975,170 | 5,660 | 273,253,480 | 26,616 | 1,284,967,248 |
| 07 | 8,777 | 529,990,368 | 6,144 | 370,999,296 | 3,010 | 181,755,840 | 3,896 | 235,256,064 | 7,940 | 479,448,960 | 10,118 | 610,965,312 | 39,885 | 2,408,415,840 |
| 08 | 6,022 | 489,696,996 | 4,108 | 334,054,344 | 2,346 | 190,772,028 | 1,852 | 150,600,936 | 4,073 | 331,208,214 | 4,686 | 381,056,148 | 23,087 | 1,877,388,666 |
| 09 | 4,042 | 381,071,676 | 2,728 | 257,190,384 | 1,312 | 123,692,736 | 1,064 | 100,311,792 | 2,559 | 241,257,402 | 3,169 | 298,766,982 | 14,874 | 1,402,290,972 |
| 10 | 2,664 | 298,581,120 | 1,764 | 197,709,120 | 841 | 94,259,280 | 685 | 76,774,800 | 1,635 | 183,250,800 | 2,112 | 236,712,960 | 9,701 | 1,087,288,080 |
| 11 | 228 | - | 135 | - | 108 | - | 110 | - | 190 | - | 245 | - | 1,016 | - |
| 12 | 1,995 | 270,785,340 | 1,350 | 183,238,200 | 449 | 60,943,668 | 430 | 58,364,760 | 918 | 124,601,976 | 1,384 | 187,853,088 | 6,526 | 885,787,032 |
| 13 | 1,194 | 179,236,116 | 841 | 126,245,874 | 270 | 40,530,780 | 224 | 33,625,536 | 462 | 69,352,668 | 618 | 92,770,452 | 3,609 | 541,761,426 |
| 14 | 804 | 129,746,304 | 479 | 77,299,104 | 185 | 29,854,560 | 138 | 22,269,888 | 285 | 45,992,160 | 352 | 56,804,352 | 2,243 | 361,966,368 |
| 15 | 520 | 97,912,880 | 253 | 47,638,382 | 156 | 29,373,864 | 133 | 25,043,102 | 244 | 45,943,736 | 257 | 48,391,558 | 1,563 | 294,303,522 |
| 16 | 211 | 43,097,172 | 114 | 23,284,728 | 107 | 21,854,964 | 86 | 17,565,672 | 136 | 27,778,272 | 109 | 22,263,468 | 763 | 155,844,276 |
| 17 | 64 | 14,285,184 | 60 | 13,392,360 | 45 | 10,044,270 | 32 | 7,142,592 | 37 | 8,258,622 | 41 | 9,151,446 | 279 | 62,274,474 |
| Total | 71,445 | 4,095,997,240 | 46,054 | 2,697,171,212 | 37,474 | 1,803,078,604 | 28,896 | 1,479,203,434 | 67,576 | 3,343,868,036 | 75,430 | 3,874,943,600 | 326,875 | 17,294,262,126 |

Source: Calculations based on the New Harmonized Public Service Salary Structure (Basic and Allowances Grade Level Step 8 as indicated in Table 5.9 below) 1999.

# Table 5.8: 122 Federal Statutory Bodies and State-owned Companies Zonal Consolidated Salary Statistics (GL 01-17) in Naira (₦)

| Grade Level (GL) | Zone 1 No. of Staff | Zone 1 Salary | Zone 2 No. of Staff | Zone 2 Salary | Zone 3 No. of Staff | Zone 3 Salary | Zone 4 No. of Staff | Zone 4 Salary | Zone 5 No. of Staff | Zone 5 Salary | Zone 6 No. of Staff | Zone 6 Salary | Total No. of Staff | Total Salary |
|---|---|---|---|---|---|---|---|---|---|---|---|---|---|---|
| 01 | 930 | 26,253,900 | 660 | 18,631,800 | 846 | 23,882,580 | 771 | 21,765,330 | 868 | 24,503,640 | 871 | 24,588,330 | 4,946 | 139,625,580 |
| 02 | 1,694 | 51,053,772 | 1,112 | 33,513,456 | 1,966 | 59,251,308 | 980 | 29,535,240 | 1,860 | 56,056,680 | 1,941 | 58,497,858 | 9,553 | 287,908,314 |
| 03 | 2,310 | 73,943,100 | 1,658 | 53,072,580 | 2,716 | 86,939,160 | 1,468 | 46,990,680 | 3,428 | 109,730,280 | 2,874 | 91,996,740 | 14,454 | 462,672,540 |
| 04 | 2,484 | 89,528,328 | 2,472 | 89,095,824 | 2,189 | 78,895,938 | 1,303 | 46,962,726 | 2,546 | 91,762,932 | 3,396 | 122,398,632 | 14,390 | 518,644,380 |
| 05 | 3,252 | 132,896,232 | 2,560 | 104,616,960 | 1,932 | 78953112 | 968 | 39,558,288 | 2,596 | 106,088,136 | 3,448 | 140,905,968 | 14,756 | 603,018,696 |
| 06 | 5,138 | 248,052,364 | 3,796 | 183,263,288 | 2,066 | 99,742,348 | 1,287 | 62,133,786 | 3,531 | 170,469,618 | 4,829 | 233,134,462 | 20,647 | 996,795,866 |
| 07 | 3,565 | 215,268,960 | 2,983 | 180,125,472 | 1,209 | 73,004,256 | 758 | 45,771,072 | 2,162 | 130,550,208 | 4,028 | 243,226,752 | 14,705 | 887,946,720 |
| 08 | 4,340 | 352,920,120 | 3,393 | 275,911,974 | 1,400 | 113,845,200 | 1,062 | 86,359,716 | 2,052 | 166,864,536 | 3,547 | 288,434,946 | 15,794 | 1,284,336,492 |
| 09 | 6,739 | 635,339,442 | 4,191 | 395,119,098 | 1,388 | 130,857,864 | 1,021 | 96,257,838 | 2,459 | 231,829,602 | 4,356 | 410,674,968 | 20,154 | 1,900,078,812 |
| 10 | 3,199 | 358,543,920 | 2,428 | 272,130,240 | 745 | 83,499,600 | 493 | 55,255,440 | 1,246 | 139,651,680 | 2,312 | 259,128,960 | 10,423 | 1,168,209,840 |
| 11 | 709 | – | 386 | – | 98 | – | 44 | – | 196 | – | 402 | – | 1,835 | – |
| 12 | 1,401 | 190,160,532 | 1,098 | 149,033,736 | 461 | 62,572,452 | 286 | 38,819,352 | 679 | 92,162,028 | 1,164 | 157,992,048 | 5,089 | 690,740,148 |
| 13 | 986 | 148,012,404 | 748 | 112,285,272 | 304 | 45,634,656 | 171 | 25,669,494 | 418 | 62,747,652 | 721 | 108,232,194 | 3,348 | 502,581,672 |
| 14 | 702 | 113,285,952 | 493 | 79,558,368 | 215 | 34,695,840 | 144 | 23,238,144 | 314 | 50,672,064 | 428 | 69,068,928 | 2,296 | 370,519,296 |
| 15 | 311 | 58,559,434 | 234 | 44,060,796 | 77 | 14,498,638 | 72 | 13,557,168 | 132 | 24,854,808 | 187 | 35,210,978 | 1,013 | 190,741,822 |
| 16 | 27 | 25,940,004 | 61 | 12,459,372 | 64 | 13,072,128 | 61 | 12,459,372 | 79 | 16,135,908 | 82 | 16,748,664 | 474 | 96,815,448 |
| 17 | 55 | 12,276,330 | 33 | 7,365,798 | 44 | 9,821,064 | 33 | 7,365,798 | 51 | 11,383,506 | 38 | 8,481,828 | 254 | 56,694,324 |
| Total | 37,942 | 2,732,034,794 | 28,306 | 2,010,244,034 | 17,720 | 1,009,166,144 | 10,922 | 651,699,444 | 24,618 | 1,485,463,278 | 34,624 | 228,772,256 | 154,132 | 10,157,329,950 |

Source: Calculations based on the New Harmonized Public Service Salary Structure (Basic and Allowances Grade Level Step 8 as indicated in Table 5.9 below) 1999.

## Table 5.9: New Harmonized Public Service Salary Structure (Basic and Allowances, Grade Level Step 8)

| Grade Level | Basic salary and allowances in Naira ₦ |
|---|---|
| 01 | 28,230 |
| 02 | 30,138 |
| 03 | 32,010 |
| 04 | 36,042 |
| 05 | 40,866 |
| 06 | 48,278 |
| 07 | 60,384 |
| 08 | 81,318 |
| 09 | 94,278 |
| 10 | 112,080 |
| 12 | 135,732 |
| 13 | 150,114 |
| 14 | 161,376 |
| 15 | 188,294 |
| 16 | 204,252 |
| 17 | 223,206 |

Source: Federal Government Salary Structure, 2004.

## References

Asiodu, P. C., 1979, 'The Civil Service: an Insider's View, in Oyeleye Oyediran' ed., *Nigerian Government and Politics under Military Rule*, London: The Macmillan Press Ltd., pp. 73-95.

Coleman, J. S., 1958, *Nigeria - Background to Nationalism*, Berkeley: University of California Press.

Dudley, B. J., 1982, *An Introduction to Nigerian Government and Politics*, London, the Macmillan Press Ltd.

Gboyega, A., 1997, 'Nigeria: Conflict Unresolved', in I. W. Zartman ed., *Governance as Conflict Management: Politics and Violence in West Africa*, Washington, D.C.: Brookings Institution Press, pp. 142-195.

Gboyega, A., 2003, 'Local Autonomy in Federal Polities: The Nigerian Local Government System in Historical Perspective', in Aaron T. Gana and Samuel G. Egwu eds., *Federalism in Africa Vol. Two: Framing the National Question*, Trenton, NJ and Asmara, Eritrea: Africa World Press, Inc., pp. 55-80.

Federal Ministry of Finance, 2000, 'National Capacity Assessment Report of the Federal Republic of Nigeria in Collaboration with the World Bank', Abuja: Federal Ministry of Finance.

Federal Republic of Nigeria, 2000, *Public Service Rules*, Lagos: Federal Government Press.

Ikime, O., 2002, 'The Nigerian Civil War and the National Question: A Historical Analysis', in Eghosa E. Osaghae, E. Nwudiwe & R.T. Suberu eds., *The Civil War and Aftermath* Ibadan: Program on Ethnic and Federal Studies, pp. 52-73.

Isumonah, V. A., 2003, 'Planned and Unplanned Outcomes: Uneven and Unsteady Pathways to Democratization in Nigeria', in Julius O. Ihonvbere and John M. Mbaku eds., *Political Liberalization and Democratization in Africa: Lessons from Country Experiences*, Westport, CT: Praeger, pp. 113-139.

Joseph, R .A., 1991, *Democracy and Prebendal Politics in Nigeria*, Ibadan: Specturm Books Ltd.

Momoh, R. A. I., 1987, 'State and Ethnic Interests', in Ukwu, I. Ukwu ed., *Federal Character and National Integration in Nigeria*, Kuru, Jos: National Institute for Policy and Strategic Studies, pp. 53-59.

Nyiam, T., 1999, 'No Easy Walk to Freedom', *Tell*, Lagos, May 3, pp. 44-47.

Olugbemi, S. O., 1979, 'The Civil Service: an Outsider's View', in Oyeleye Oyediran ed., *Nigerian Government and Politics under Military Rule*, London: The Macmillan Press Ltd., pp. 73-95.

Onajide, M.O., 1979, 'The Civil Service – Some Comments' in Ladipo Adamolekun and Alex Gboyega eds., *Leading Issues in Nigerian Public Service,* Ile-Ife: University of Ife Press, pp. 26-35.

Schwarz, W., 1968, *Nigeria*, London: Pall Mall Press.

Sklar, R. L., 1963, 'Nigerian Political Parties: Power in an Emergent African Nation', Princeton: Princeton University Press.

Suberu, R. T., 2004, 'Pseudo-Federalism and the Political Crisis of Revenue Allocation', in Adigun A. B. Agbaje, Larry Diamond and Ebere Onwudiwe eds, *Nigeria's Struggle for Democracy and Good Governance: a Festschrift for Oyeleye Oyediran,* Ibadan: University Press, pp. 29-46.

# 6

# The Distribution of Health Benefits

Roman Catholic missionaries formally introduced the Western care system in Nigeria when they established the Sacred Heart Hospital in Abeokuta in the 1860s (see All Refer). European traders had brought its rudimentary elements before then. The missionaries set up hospitals in areas where their activities were relatively popular, beginning at the coast and later in the hinterlands. The precursor role that European traders and missionaries are believed to have played for colonizers has often led some to trace institutions that originated with the former to the latter. Hence Alubo (2001:314) writes that 'the Western heath care system in Nigeria is a colonial legacy.' Records show that the first colonial government hospitals were sited in 'Lagos, Calabar and other coastal trading centres in 1870s' (ibid).

'Today, Western medical services are available from three sources: public (federal, state, and local governments), private and voluntary agencies or missionary sources' (Alubo 2001:314). There is a wide variation in the distribution of medical personnel and hospital facilities by which the availability of heath care services can be measured (Kirk-Greene 1970). The statistics of these are segmented. For example, Okafor (1982) is concerned with the distribution of hospitals in Bendel State (now divided into Edo and Delta states) in terms of rural-urban shares and doctor-population ratios. While statistics of government and missionary health facilities could be collected, it is almost impossible to do so for private facilities, most of which are 'operating without appropriate licensure by State Ministries of Health' (Ogubenkun et al. 1999:174).

However, available records indicate that there were 118 mission hospitals with only 25 in the entire north and 101 government hospitals in Nigeria by independence in 1960. 'By 1979 there were 562 general hospitals, supplemented by 16 maternity and/or pediatric hospitals, 11 armed forces hospitals, 6 teaching hospitals, and 3 prison hospitals. In addition, general health centres were estimated to total slightly less than 600; general clinics 2,740; maternity homes 930; and maternal health centers 1,240. By 1985, there were 84 health establishments owned by the federal government, 3,023 owned by state governments and 1,436 privately owned establishments.' (http://reference.allrefer.com/country-guide-staudy/nigeria74.html).

The distribution of ownership of hospitals between government and private is relevant to the analysis of social welfare because the latter have either been driven by profit or cost effectiveness. This is regardless of the crisis triggered by reduced federal expenditure 'from an average of 3.5 per cent in the early 1970s to less than 2 per cent in the 1980s and 1990s' in the public health sector, resulting in partial or total closures, and short supplies in material and personnel (Ogunbekun et al. 1999:175). Another relevance of the distribution lies in the fact that 'in modern Nigeria, church-run facilities are numerous and seen to be distributed more evenly between urban and rural areas *than public sector facilities*' (emphasis added, Alubo 2001:316). Thus, the location of a government health facility makes some difference to the people in terms of a community's share of government social welfare benefit.

### Table 6.1: Distribution of Federal Government-owned Teaching and Specialist Hospitals and Medical Centres as at 1996

| Zone | Number per State | Zonal Total |
|------|------------------|-------------|
| 1 | Ekiti (0), Lagos (3), Ogun (2), Ondo (1), Osun (1), Oyo (1) | 8 |
| 2 | Abia (1), Anambra (1), Ebonyi (0), Enugu (3), Imo (1) | 6 |
| 3 | Jigawa (0), Kaduna (2), Kano (2), Katsina (1), Kebbi (0), Sokoto (2), Zamfara (0) | 7 |
| 4 | Adamawa (0), Bauchi (0), Borno (2), Gombe (1), Taraba (0), Yobe (0) | 3 |
| 5 | Benue (1), Kogi (0), Kwara (1), Nassarawa (0), Niger (2), Plateau (1), FCT(1) | 6 |
| 6 | Akwa Ibom (0), Bayelsa (0), Cross River (2), Delta (0), Edo (3), Rivers (1) | 6 |
| | Total | 36 |

Source: Federal Ministry of Health 1996 Annual Calendar.

Note: Index of composition of zones

| Zone | Constituent States |
|------|--------------------|
| 1 | Ekiti, Lagos, Ogun, Ondo, Osun, Oyo |
| 2 | Abia, Anambra, Ebonyi, Enugu, Imo |
| 3 | Jigawa, Kaduna, Kano, Katsina, Kebbi. Sokoto, Zamfara |
| 4 | Adamawa, Bauchi, Borno, Gombe, Taraba, Yobe |
| 5 | Benue, Kogi, Kwara, Nassarawa, Niger, Plateau, FCT |
| 6 | Akwa Ibom, Bayelsa, Cross River, Delta, Edo, Rivers |

In Table 6.1, the South-West shows up as the leading beneficiary in the distribution of Federal Government-owned teaching and specialist hospitals and medical centres. It is followed by the North-West and other zones in equal share except the North-East which comes far behind by half.

The South-West takes the lead position in federal capital expenditure on health from Table 6.2. It took double the North-Central's and more than double the North East's. It is followed by the North-West, South-East and South-South respectively. It is difficult to fathom the reason for the exceedingly high share of the North-West relative to other zones. The only pointer to this is that in 1995 (under the presidency of General Sani Abacha who hails from Kano) Bayero University Teaching Hospital, Kano, in this zone, received more than triple the average allocation of all federal medical centres. However, the south as a region took ₦3.6 billion (57.4 per cent) to the north's ₦2.7 billion (42.6 per cent).

## Table 6.2: Ministry of Health Capital Expenditure, 1995-2001
### (₦ millions)

| S/N | Name of Institution | Zone 1 | Zone 2 | Zone 3 | Zone 4 | Zone 5 | Zone 6 |
|---|---|---|---|---|---|---|---|
| 1 | UCH, Ibadan | 342.0 | | | | | |
| 2 | LUTH, Lagos | 265.6 | | | | | |
| 3 | ABUTH, Zaria | | | 429.0 | | | |
| 4 | UNTH, Enugu | | 427.0 | | | | |
| 5 | UBTH, Benin city | | | | | | 263.6 |
| 6 | OAUTH, lle-ife | 265.6 | | | | | |
| 7 | UITH, Ilorin | | | | | 269.6 | |
| 8 | JUTH, Jos | | | | | 265.6 | |
| 9 | UPTH, PH | | | | | | 265.6 |
| 10 | UCTH, Calabar | | | | | | 269.8 |
| 11 | UMTH, Maiduguri | | | | 342.0 | | |
| 12 | UDTH, Sokoto | | | 264.6 | | | |
| 13 | Bayero UTH, Kano | | | 346.6 | | | |
| 14 | NAUTH, Nnewi | | 265.6 | | | | |
| 15 | NOH, Enugu | | 125.3 | | | | |
| 16 | NOH, Dala Kano | | | 128.8 | | | |
| 17 | Psychiatric Hosp., Yaba | 77.6 | | | | | |
| 18 | Psychiatric Hosp., Benin city | | | | | | 75.0 |
| 19 | Psychiatric Hosp., Abeokuta | 77.6 | | | | | |
| 20 | Fed. Specialist Hospital, Gwagwalada | | | | | 199.7 | |
| 21 | FMC, Umuahia | | 122.3 | | | | |
| 22 | NOH, Lagos | 203.7 | | | | | |
| 23 | FMC, Owo | 138.2 | | | | | |
| 24 | FMC, Suleja | | | | | | |
| 25 | FMC, Abeokuta | 107.2 | | | | | |
| 26 | Federal Specialist Hosp., Irrua | | | | | | 64.2 |
| 27 | FMC, Minna | | | | | 128.2 | |
| 28 | FMC, Owerri | | 104.2 | | | | |
| 29 | FMC, Makurdi | | | | | 71.2 | |
| 30 | FMC, Kastina | | | 114.2 | | | |
| 31 | FMC, Gombe | | | | 118.7 | | |
| 32 | Psychiatric Hosp., Enugu | | 62.1 | | | | |
| 33 | Psychiatric Hosp., Kaduna | | | 62.1 | | | |
| 34 | Psychiatric Hosp., Calabar | | | | | | 62.1 |
| 35 | Psychiatric Hosp., Maidugri | | | | 62.1 | | |
| 36 | Psychiatric Hosp., Sokoto | | | 62.1 | | | |
| Total | | 1,477.5 | 1,106.5 | 1,407.4 | 522.8 | 734.6??? | 1,000.3 |

Source: Federal Government Budgets, various years.

The zonal distribution of federal recurrent expenditure on health in Table 3 shows a slight reverse to the distribution of capital expenditure. As in previous distributions, the South-West is in the lead by factors of almost 2.2 and 4.7. South-South beat the North-West to the second position by a significant margin. Again, the south as a region took the larger share of ₦2,2361.2 million (63.7 per cent) to the north's ₦1,2752.1 (36.3 per cent) million.

## Table 6.3: Ministry of Health Recurrent Expenditure, 1995-2001 (₦ millions)

| S/N | Name of Institute | Zone 1 | Zone 2 | Zone 3 | Zone 4 | Zone 5 | Zone 6 |
|---|---|---|---|---|---|---|---|
| 1 | UCH, Ibadan | 2,420.1 | | | | | |
| 2 | LUTH, Lagos | 2,353.6 | | | | | |
| 3 | ABUTH, Zaria | | | 2,057.8 | | | |
| 4 | UNTH, Enugu | | 2,089.9 | | | | |
| 5 | UBTH, Benin city | | | | | | 1,959.4 |
| 6 | OAUTH, lle-ife | 1,925.5 | | | | | |
| 7 | UITH, Ilorin | | | | | 1,477.5 | 1,544.9 |
| 8 | JUTH, Jos | | | | | 1,378.4 | |
| 9 | UPTH, PH | | | | | | |
| 10 | UCTH, Calabar | | | | | | 1,379.1 |
| 11 | UMTH, Maiduguri | | | | 1,572.1 | | |
| 12 | UDTH, Sokoto | | | 1,109.4 | | | |
| 13 | Bayero UTH, Kano | | | 771.4 | | | |
| 14 | NAUTH, Nnewi | | 897.4 | | | | |
| 15 | NOH, Enugu | | 519.11 | | | | |
| 16 | NOH, Dala Kano | | | 768.2 | | | |
| 17 | Psychiatric Hosp., Yaba | 1,149.8 | | | | | |
| 18 | Psychiatric Hosp., Benin city | | | | | | 1,250.8 |
| 19 | Psychiatric Hosp., Abeokuta | 712.3 | | | | | |
| 20 | Fed. Specialist Hospital, Gwagwalada | | | | | 1,262.1 | |
| 21 | FMC, Umuahia | | 664.6 | | | | |
| 22 | NOH, Lagos | 1,188.8 | | | | | |
| 23 | FMC, Owo | 389.4 | | | | | |
| 24 | FMC, Suleja | | | | | 50.22 | |
| 25 | FMC, Abeokuta | 398.5 | | | | | |
| 26 | Federal Specialist Hosp., Irrua | | | | | | 386.1 |
| 27 | FMC, Minna | | | | | 47.63 | |
| 28 | FMC, Owerri | | 537.0 | | | | |
| 29 | FMC, Makurdi | | | | | 434.8 | |
| 30 | FMC, Kastina | | | 318.3 | | | |
| 31 | FMC, Gombe | | | | 353.6 | | |
| 32 | Psychiatric Hosp., Enugu | | 306.5 | | | | |
| 33 | Psychiatric Hosp., Kaduna | | | 294.3 | | | |
| 34 | Psychiatric Hosp., Calabar | | | | | | 288.4 |
| 35 | Psychiatric Hosp., Maiduguri | | | | 285.5 | 285.5 | |
| 36 | Psychiatric Hosp, Sokoto | | | 285.4 | | | |
| Total | | 10,538.0 | 5,014.5 | 5,604.8 | 2,211.2 | 4,936.1 | 6,808.7 |

Source: Federal Government Budgets, various years

## References

Alubo, O., 2001, 'The promise and limits of private medicine: health policy dilemmas in Nigeria', *Health Policy and Planning.* Vol. 16, No. 3, pp. 313-321.

Ogunbekun, I., Adenike Ogunbeku and Nosa Orobaton, 1999, 'Private health care in Nigeria: walking the tightrope', *Health Policy and Planning*, Vol. 14, No. 2: 174-181.

Okafor, S.I., 1982, 'Policy and practice: the case of medical facilities in Nigeria', *Social Science and Medicine,* Vol. 16, No. 22, pp. 1971-77.

# 7

## Federal Expenditure on Roads, Housing and Erosion Control

Nigeria's principal modes of transportation as elsewhere are water, rail, and road. This chapter focuses on road transportation for reasons that are identified below. Scholars have told the history of transport development in different ways (Ikporukpo 1998:136). However, all are agreed that it is synonymous with colonial influence and interests. It is not surprising that the transport structure, the north-south route excluding lateral east-west connections, was fashioned according to the economic interests of the British colonialists. It began from the development of seaports with railway routes shooting from some of them into the hinterlands. 'Lateral interconnections and feeder routes' followed much later (Ikporukpo 1998:136).

Thus, 'the location of some economically important resources such as cocoa, groundnut, palm oil, and mineral resources largely determined the routing of extent of transport networks in the country' (Filani 1981:210). Such economic considerations naturally favoured certain coastal towns and urban centres which enjoyed a disproportionate share of transport networks against other towns and particularly the rural areas. As Filani (1981:210) wrote, 'the initial lavational advantages enjoyed by certain areas through the colonial transport networks have been reinforced and extended, even after twenty-one years of political independence.'

The first post-independence government tended to continue with the 'inherited transport networks' and to extend it. This can be seen from the emphasis of transport development on inter-city linkages and evacuation routes. Allocations to the transport sector in the First (1962-1968), Second (1970-1974) and Third (1975-1980) National Development Plans were 21.per cent, 24.4 per cent and 27.5 per cent respectively. Transport sub-sector allocations in the Third National Development Plan were: land (₦6.23 billion, 85 per cent), air (₦528.0 million, 7.2 per cent) and water (₦545.62 million, 7.5 per cent). From these figures, it is obvious that road development has received the greatest attention of the government and, therefore, deserves a special focus. The road transport sub-sector is also focused on because it is the dominant mode of transportation in Nigeria. Indeed, it is estimated that it represents 90 per cent of the total volume of transportation.

In Nigeria, only the government provides modern roads and, until recently, communication facilities. The sole responsibility of the government for the provision of roads is explained mainly by 'the huge capital outlay required, practicability, colonial history and current political advantages' (Central Bank of Nigeria 1994). The deplorable conditions of the majority of Nigerian highways and roads at most times significantly accounts for the high rate of road accidents (Odeleye, mimeo). Table 1 shows sizes of states and Federal Capital Territory. It is clear from this table that there is a wide variation in the sizes of states. Thus, Table 2 shows a general correlation between lengths of federal roads by type in the states and sizes of the states.

**Table 7.1: Area of Nigeria State by State (including) FCT Abuja**

| Serial Number | State | Area (square kilometers) |
|---|---|---|
| 1 | Abia | 6,320 |
| 2 | Adamawa | 36,917 |
| 3 | Akwa Ibom | 7,081 |
| 4 | Anambra | 4,844 |
| 5 | Bauchi | 64,6055 |
| 6 | Benue | 34,059 |
| 7 | Borno | 70,898 |
| 8 | Cross River | 20,156 |
| 9 | Delta | 17,698 |
| 10 | Edo | 17,802 |
| 11 | Enugu | 12,831 |
| 12 | Imo | 5,530 |
| 13 | Jigawa | 23,154 |
| 14 | Kaduna | 46,053 |
| 15 | Kano | 20,131 |
| 16 | Kastina | 24,192 |
| 17 | Kebbi | 36,800 |
| 18 | Kogi | 29,833 |
| 19 | Kwara | 36,825 |
| 20 | Lagos | 3,345 |
| 21 | Niger | 76,363 |
| 22 | Ogun | 16,762 |
| 23 | Ondo | 20,959 |
| 24 | Osun | 9,251 |
| 25 | Oyo | 28,454 |
| 26 | Plateau | 58,030 |
| 27 | Rivers | 21,850 |
| 28 | Sokoto | 65,735 |
| 29 | Taraba | 54,473 |
| 30 | Yobe | 45,502 |
| 31 | Abuja (FCT) | 7,315 |
| Total | | 923,768 |

Source: Federal Ministry of Works & Housing, *Digest of Statistics*, 1999.

## Table 7.2: Length of Federal Roads as at 1996

| State | Asphaltic Concrete (km) | Surface Concrete (km) | Gravel on Earth (km) | Total Length (km) |
|---|---|---|---|---|
| Abia | 296.00 | 221.00 | 19.00 | 536.00 |
| Adamawa | 612.00 | 204.00 | 492.00 | 1,308.00 |
| Akwa Ibom | 334.00 | 171.00 | 40.00 | 545.00 |
| Anambra | 540.00 | 133.00 | 32.00 | 549.00 |
| Bauchi | 1,227.00 | 198.00 | 353.00 | 1,778.00 |
| Benue | 592.00 | 203.00 | 292.00 | 1,087.00 |
| Borno | 1,036.00 | 358.00 | 787.00 | 2,181.00 |
| Cross River | 722.35 | 196.80 | 130.04 | 1,049.19 |
| Delta | 605.50 | 37.00 | 38.00 | 680.50 |
| Edo | 641.50 | 112.00 | - | 753.50 |
| Enugu | 522.00 | 215.00 | - | 777.00 |
| Imo | 344.00 | 163.00 | - | 507.00 |
| Jigawa | 576.00 | 80.00 | 72.00 | 728.00 |
| Kaduna | 1,516.00 | 150.00 | 8.00 | 1,674.00 |
| Kano | 720.00 | 165.00 | - | 885.00 |
| Kastina | 495.00 | 292.00 | 55.00 | 842.00 |
| Kebbi | 248.40 | 325.00 | 262.00 | 835.40 |
| Kogi | 500.00 | 441.00 | 232.00 | 1,173.00 |
| Kwara | 357.00 | 271.00 | 262.00 | 890.00 |
| Lagos | 438.66 | - | - | 438.66 |
| Niger | 909.00 | 743.00 | 396.00 | 2,048.00 |
| Ogun | 953.00 | 95.00 | - | 1,048.00 |
| Ondo | 662.00 | 285.00 | - | 947.00 |
| Osun | 320.70 | 183.00 | - | 503.70 |
| Oyo | 314.20 | 346.00 | 266.00 | 928.20 |
| Plateau | 846.50 | 388.50 | 560.00 | 1,795.00 |
| Rivers | 397.00 | 157.00 | 147.00 | 701.00 |
| Sokoto | 356.00 | 764.00 | 427.00 | 1,547.00 |
| Taraba | 564.00 | 357.00 | 703.00 | 1,624.00 |
| Yobe | 341.00 | 317.00 | 152.00 | 810.00 |
| Abuja (FCT) | 158.00 | 58.60 | 20.00 | 236.60 |
| Zamfara | - | - | - | - |
| Ebonyi | 160.00 | 295.00 | 100.00 | 555.00 |
| Bayelsa | - | - | - | - |
| Ekiti | - | - | - | - |
| Gombe | - | - | - | - |
| Nasarawa | - | - | - | - |

Source: Federal Ministry of Works and Housing Digest of Statistics 1994-997.

While the per capita expenditure in city roads in Nigeria is, compared with other countries of the world, to say the least, insignificant as shown in Table 3 below, it is worthwhile to investigate the spatial distribution of federal government expenditure on both inter and intra-city roads against the background of past studies. In his study of government investments in the transport sector from 1945 to 1975, Ogunjumo (1983:177) concluded that ethnic consideration does not explain 'the location quotients of the federal roads in Ibadan, Onitsha and Owerri provinces' but that administrative or political expediency and demographic factors of population and land area command a greater weight in the explanation of federal road investment.

### Table 7.3: Per capita Expenditure in City Roads and Other Indicators

| City | Travel time (minutes) | Car ownership cars/1,000 | Road capital expenditure ($) |
|------|------|------|------|
| Lagos, Nigeria | 85.00 | 4.30 | 0.04 |
| Cairo, Egypt | 59.00 | 50.10 | 5.70 |
| Paris, France | 35.00 | 426.00 | 248.00 |
| New York, USA | 36.50 | 232.00 | 123.22 |

Source: UNCHS (Habitat) Global Urban Indicators Database, 1996.

However the zonal shares of federal road expenditure between 1995 and 2000 shown in Table 4 indicate that the north, comprising zones 3, 4 and 5 took the greater share. In particular, zone 3, the north central zone, which held the office of the head of state during this period, has the highest zonal share. The South-South zone's highest share all through the years was buoyed by special agencies: the Oil Mineral Producing Areas Development Commission (OMPADEC) and Niger Delta Development Commission (NDDC) that the federal government created to cushion the effects of oil exploitation.

### Table 7.4: Approved Budgets on Roads, 1995-2000

| Zone | 1995 | 1996 | 1997 | 1998 | 1999 | 2000 | Total |
|------|------|------|------|------|------|------|------|
| 1 | 402,500,000 | 121,452,500 | 360,000,000 | 359,000,000 | 220,000,000 | 2,573,743,153 | 4,036,695,653 |
| 2 | 440,000,000 | 184,902,500 | 234,800,000 | 420,000,000 | 180,000,000 | 4,816,077,477 | 6,275,779,977 |
| 3 | 644,000,000 | 307,732,500 | 661,775,980 | 665,000,000 | 1,275,000,000 | 5,503,000,000 | 9,056,508,480 |
| 4 | 402,000,000 | 199,656,000 | 200,000,000 | 173,000,000 | 435,000,000 | 5,806,990,908 | 7,216,646,908 |
| 5 | 403,000,000 | 259,510,500 | 347,000,000 | 1,029,000,000 | 380,000,000 | 2,855,000,000 | 5,273,510,500 |
| 6 | 719,000,000 | 446,824,900 | 1,199,800,000 | 3,059,000,000 | 2,945,000,000 | 10,090,088,162 | 15,723,715,062 |

Source: Federal Government's Approved Budget Estimates, various issues.

Notes: Index of Composition of Zones

| Zone | Constituent States |
|------|------|
| 1 | Ekiti, Lagos, Ogun, Ondo, Osun, Oyo |
| 2 | Abia, Anambra, Ebonyi, Enugu, Imo |
| 3 | Jigawa, Kaduna, Kano, Katsina, Kebbi, Sokoto, Zamfara |
| 4 | Adamawa, Bauchi, Borno, Gombe, Taraba, Yobe |
| 5 | Benue, Kogi, Kwara, Nassarawa, Niger, Plateau, FCT |
| 6 | Akwa Ibom, Bayelsa, Cross River, Delta, Edo, Rivers |

# Table 7.5: Federal Expenditure on Flood and Erosion Control, 1985-1996

| S/No. | Project title and location | Zone 1 | Zone 2 | Zone 3 | Zone 4 | Zone 5 | Zone 6 | Total |
|---|---|---|---|---|---|---|---|---|
| 1. | Bar beach, Victoria Island, Lagos State | 224,419,292.84 | | | | | | 224,419,292.84 |
| 2. | Einong group of villages, Cross River State | | | | | | 17,349,762.31 | 17,349,762.31 |
| 3. | Bomadi, Delta State | | | | | | 43,573,848.45 | 43,573,848.45 |
| 4. | Patani, Delta State | | | | | | 193,210,343.15 | 193,210,343.15 |
| 5. | Ijebu-Ode, Ogun State | 7,630,147.40 | | | | | | 7,630,147.40 |
| 6. | Kotangora, Niger State | | | | | 12,435,696.49 | | 12,435,696.49 |
| 7. | Ekenobiri, Unopara Umuahia, Abia State | | 9,953,462.81 | | | | | 9,953,462.81 |
| 8. | Ediba, Cross River State | | | | | | 14,947,918.70 | 14,947,918.70 |
| 9. | Nigeria Army Amphibious Training Wing, Calabar, Cross River State | | | | | | 25,195,692.43 | 25,195,692.43 |
| 10. | EPZ, Calabar, Cross River State | | | | | | 83,725,801.60 | 83,725,801.60 |
| 11. | Songare, Rivers State | | | | | | 20,945,173.90 | 20,945,173.90 |
| 12. | Bar Beach, Victoria Island, Lagos | 18,572,340.90 | | | | | | 18,572,340.90 |
| 13. | Keffi, Plateau State | | | | | 6,942,340.03 | | 6,942,340.03 |
| 14. | Ilorin, Kwara State | | | | | 5,029,908.77 | | 5,029,908.77 |
| | Total | 250,621,781.14 | 9,953,462.81 | - | - | 24,407,945.29 | 308,948,540.54 | 683,931,729.78 |

Source: Federal Ministry of Works & Housing, *Digest of Statistics*, 1999.

## Table 7.6: Federal Housing Distribution (1983-1994) in Units

| S/No. | Location | Zone 1 | Zone 2 | Zone 3 | Zone 4 | Zone 5 | Zone 6 | Total |
|---|---|---|---|---|---|---|---|---|
| 1 | Festac Town, Lagos, Lagos State | 11,438 | | | | | | 11,438 |
| 2 | Ipaja Estate, Lagos, Lagos State | 3,044 | | | | | | 3,044 |
| 3 | Sharada Estate, Kano, Kano State | | | | 178 | | | 178 |
| 4 | Aladinma & Egbeade Estate, Imo State | | 186 | | | | | 186 |
| 5 | Runji Sambo Estate, Sokoto, Sokoto State | | | 175 | | | | 175 |
| 6 | North Bank Estate, Makurdi, Benue State | | | | | 218 | | 218 |
| 7 | Bosso Estate, Minna, Niger State | | | | | 280 | | 280 |
| 8 | Trans Amadi/Rumueme Estate, Port Harcourt, Rivers State | | | | | | 207 | 207 |
| 9 | Karu Estate, Abuja, Federal Capital Territory | | | | | 251 | | 251 |
| 10 | Kubwa Estate, Abuja, Federal Capital Territory | | | | | 1,316 | | 1,316 |
| 11 | Maitama Estate, Abuja, Federal Capital Territory | | | | | 479 | | 479 |
| 12 | Asokoro Estate, Abuja, Federal Capital Territory | | | | | 144 | | 144 |
| 13 | Iguosa Estate, Benin City Edo State | | | | | | 162 | 162 |
| 14 | Gonin-gora Estate, Kaduna, Kaduna State | | | 150 | | | | 150 |
| 15 | Karu Estate, Abuja, Federal Capital Territory | | | | | 251 | | 251 |
| 16 | Kubwa Estate, Abuja, Federal Capital Territory | | | | | 188 | | 188 |
| 17 | Gubi Dan Estate, Bauchi, Bauchi State | | | | 235 | | | 235 |
| 18 | Baga Road Estate, Maiduguri, Borno State | | | | 91 | | | 91 |
| 19 | Aladinma Estate, Imo State | | 16 | | | | | 16 |
| 20 | Egbeada Estate, Owerri, Imo State | | 171 | | | | | 171 |
| 21 | Kaduna/Abuja Road Estate, Kaduna State | | | 170 | | | | 170 |
| 22 | Sharada Phase 1 Estate, Kano, Kano State | | | 171 | | | | 171 |
| 23 | Kulende Estate, Ilorin, Kwara State | | | | | 222 | | 222 |
| 24 | Obada-Oke Road Estate, Abeokuta, Ogun State | 269 | | | | | | 269 |
| 25 | Akure/Ilesha Road Estate, Akure, Ondo State | 133 | | | | | | 133 |
| 26 | Ado-Ekiti/Ikare Road Estate, Ado-Ekiti, Ekiti State | 10 | | | | | | 10 |
| 27 | Off Ikirun Bye Pass Estate, Oshogbo, Osun State | 243 | | | | | | 243 |
| 28 | Rumueme Estate, Port Harcourt, Rivers State | | | | | | 142 | 142 |
| 29 | Ruyin Sambo Estate, Sokoto, Sokoto State | | | 65 | | | | 65 |
| 30 | Ruyin Sambo Estate, Sokoto, Sokoto State | | | 150 | | | | 150 |
| | Total | 15,137 | 373 | 1,059 | 544 | 3,349 | 673 | 21,135 |

Source: Federal Ministry of Works & Housing, *Digest of Statistics*, 1999.

The distribution of federal expenditure on erosion control in Table 5, which shows non-expenditure in the North-West and North-Central, reflects the distribution of the problem itself. The question really is whether the distribution of expenditure reflects the distribution of the gravity of the problem across Nigeria. It is curious, for example, to observe in Table 5 that the North-Central took a higher share than the South-East, which studies dating back to the colonial times showed to be plagued by and prone to serious water erosion (see for example, Grove 1951). The North-West and North-East are compensated for their non-share of erosion control expenditure by federal expenditure on desertification of which they are exclusive beneficiaries.

The South-West's far greatest share of housing units derives from the status Lagos had for a long time as federal capital territory. A great many of the housing units were built by the federal government for the 1977 Arts and Culture Festival hosted in Lagos. The same explanation holds for the North-Central's impressive share. It presently hosts the capital of Nigeria and in that capacity hosted the 8th All-Africa Games in 2003, which necessitated the construction of a great many housing units in Abuja. It is difficult to make out the wide variations between the South-East and the North-West, which had both been hosts to the capitals of Regional Governments at Kaduna and Enugu respectively.

### References

Central Bank of Nigeria, *Annual Reports,*1994.

Filani, M. O., 1981, 'Towards More Efficient Transport Networks in Nigeria', *The Nigerian Journal of Economic and Social Studies*, Vol. 23, No. 2, pp. 209-224.

Grove, A. T., 1951, 'Soil Erosion and Population Problems in South-East Nigeria', *The Geographical Journal*, Vol. 117, No. 3, pp. 291-304.

Ikporupko, C. O., 1998, 'Transport Studies', in Olusegun Areola and Stanley I. Okafor eds., *50 Years of Geography in Nigeria: The Ibadan Story*, Ibadan: Ibadan University Press, pp. 135-156.

Odeleye, J. A., (n.d), *Improved Road Traffic Environment for Better Child Safety in Nigeria* - 13th ICTCT workshop.

Ogunjumo, A., 1983, 'Alternative Frameworks for Understanding the Patterns of Transportation Development in Nigeria', *The Nigerian Geographical Journal*, Vol. 26, Nos. 1&2, pp. 171-197.

Steel, R. W., Raeburn, C., Dixey, F., Masefield, G. B., Harrison Church, R. J., Jones, G. I., Stamp, L. D. and Grove, A. T., 1951, 'Soil Erosion and Population Problems in South-East Nigeria: Discussion', *The Geographical Journal*, Vol. 117, No. 3, pp. 304-306.

# 8

## Conclusion

Most southern ethno-political groups see centralization as an undifferentiated whole and have tended to reject it outright. On the contrary, this study shows that the centralization of resources in Nigeria has two aspects, namely, the sole power of the centre (federal government) to collect major revenues for sharing between itself and states and local governments (inter-governmental transfers) on the one hand, and the large chunk of revenues the federal government retains and expends at its discretion on the other. Northern groups show some awareness of this by favouring centralization to the extent that it is for inter-governmental sharing; this is understandable because the criteria used for sharing suit them. Hence, their state governments have joined southern state governments in calling for a revision of the intergovernmental sharing formula. It has, nevertheless, not been too easy for the north to make the distinction referred to above because of its grip on political power especially prior to 1999.

Then, northern ethno-political groups favoured centralization because of the belief that it was altogether beneficial to them. They believed further that all they needed to get as much of the centralized resources as they could for themselves was the control of federal political power. This is why they held on to it for as long as they could until 1999 and are battling to regain it in 2007 (Isumonah 2003). In this regard, their slogan is 'Return power to the north'. Their belief in centralization is notwithstanding their perception that they receive less than their southern ethno-political groups' share of resources that the federal government dispenses at its discretion. Similarly, the north's decades of tenacious hold on federal political power leads southern groups to think that the centralization of resources is entirely unbeneficial to them. As a result, they have been indifferent to the unsubstantiated reference by northern groups to their greater share in the benefits of federal spending.

While the winners and losers of centralization for intergovernmental sharing are very evident, this is not the case regarding centralization for the provision of services by federal government. Sharing on the basis of equality of states (40 per cent) and population (30 per cent) means that ethno-regional groups that have more states automatically receive more from inter-governmental transfers. Table

1 shows the northern region's greater net gain from intergovernmental transfer on account of the steady disproportionate increase in its number of states and local governments between 1979 and 1985. The picture becomes clearer when a unit such as Rivers State (prior to 1996) or Bendel State (prior to 1991) is considered in terms of an ethno-regional group's access to centralized resources distributed on the basis of states and local government councils as mathematically represented below (Agiobenebo 2003).

Taking 1967 as the baseline of equity, each of these states got less than one portion in the states' share of the federation account between 1976 and 1991 for Bendel State and 1976 and 1996 for Rivers State even though they were the source of the bulk of it, because of their restriction to one unit and sparing growth in the number of their local governments in relation to the rest of Nigeria especially the northern part. The diminution in any of these states' real share is the concomitant of state reorganization of Nigeria from 12 in 1967 to 19 in 1976; to 21 in 1987; to 30 in 1991 (for Bendel) and to 36 in 1996 (for Rivers).

| 1967 | 1976 | 1987 | 1991 | 1991 | 1996 |
|------|------|------|------|------|------|
| $1/12$ | $1/19$ | $1/21$ | $1/30$(Rivers) | $2/30=1/15$ | (Bendel) $2/36=$ $1/18$ (Rivers) |

## Table 8.1: Regional Shares of Statutory and Non-statutory Allocations of Revenue, 1979-85 (Per Cent of Total)

| Region | 1979 | 1980 | 1981 | 1982 | 1983 | 1984 | 1985 |
|--------|------|------|------|------|------|------|------|
| Northern | 47.2 | 46.5 | 50.9 | 50.3 | 49.2 | 49.4 | 53.9 |
| Eastern | 25.8 | 26.4 | 23.4 | 23.5 | 23.1 | 22.6 | 22.1 |
| Western | 18.1 | 17.9 | 18.2 | 19.8 | 19.3 | 19.1 | 16.5 |
| Mid-Western | 8.8 | 9.3 | 7.3 | 6.6 | 6.5 | 6.7 | 6.3 |
| Total (%) | 100.0 | 100.0 | 100.0 | 100.0 | 100.0 | | |
| Total ( m) | 2,903.5 | 3,812.9 | 4,910.6 | 4,258.4 | 4,236.7 | 3,926.6 | 4,671.7 |

Source: Aleman Eduardo & Daniel Treisman (2002), 'Fiscal Politics in "Ethnically-Mined", Developing, Federal States: Central Strategies and Secessionist Violence', paper presented at San Diego workshop.

Thus, the costs and benefits of inter-regional transfers are well known, self-evident and need no substantiation. It is the distribution of the benefits of retained resources by the centre to geo-ethnic groups that has needed validation since even apparent gainers have tended to deny they are. Such a denial by a South-West's federal minister prompted the Federal Character Commission to publish the geo-ethnic composition of the federal civil service, statutory bodies and state-owned companies in 1999 (*This Day*, Lagos, 4 October 1999). Thus, how these resources are distributed constitutes the issue of federal presence and was the focus of this study, which set out to determine the veracity of claims and counter-claims between ethno-political groups about their gainers and losers. It was in an attempt to unravel the other side of the coin of resource allocation in Nigeria.

The various ways the federal government distributes its retained resources between different parts of the federation are captured by the expression 'federal spending'. This is probably what Bienen (1983:145) meant when he wrote 'direct federal spending in the states has become increasingly important as compared to revenue allocations, but it is hard to measure the importance of such spending'. While this study has not measured all such spending, it has at least provided an absolute value of aspects of it employing the money-flow approach, which as Odufalu (1983) argued, is very appropriate where there is a great concern about the inter-regional distribution of benefits. Thus, it has filled part of the gap in the literature by analyzing the spatial patterns of federal presence and helped to establish a more accurate gain-loss calculus. It has shown that federal presence is an important measure of centralized resources. When Bayelsa State, a core oil-producing region was created in 1996, there was no single federal infrastructure – road, institution of higher learning, hospital, industry, etc. located within the state. Indeed, many of the complaints of agitated youths are about lack of these amenities and make it plausible to argue that had there been adequate federal presence in these states, youth restiveness would not have arisen. Barring greed, accurate knowledge of the distribution of federal presence is useful for reducing the feeling of unfair treatment of real regional gainers in the distribution of resources while at the same time giving them reason to empathize with losers especially those groups that bear the brunt of the negative externalities of producing the resources that are shared between tiers of governments.

From the various chapters on ethno-political groups' share of resources, the South-West is unmistakably the greatest gainer of federal presence, that is, from the distribution of resources which the centre retains. The South-South fares very well contrary to received knowledge. In terms of regional comparison, the south is the greater gainer than the north. This probably wholly or partly explains the north's belief in federal political power to guarantee it some leverage. The South's grumbling could in the same vein be understood as being borne out of conceiving centralization as an undifferentiated whole.

Given these findings, where lies the power of allocation of what the federal government retains? Is it headship of the state or influence in the civil service? It is important to note that the distribution of the types of resources focused by this study is guided by some unalterable criteria, which benefit those with the advantage of a head start or drive. With regards to the distribution of primary and secondary educational facilities, location advantage initially derived from natural proximity to the coast 'urbanization and trade, migration and European settlement, the development of transport network, the spread of cash crop and emergence of new occupational structures' (Anusionwu 1980:3). The South-West's greatest benefit could be understood to a large extent in these lights. Evidence of its stronger presence in the topmost cadres of the civil service and public corporations may also suggest the significance of policy making influence, going by the logic of regional competition for resources, in its greatest share of federal presence.

The South-South's rising performance in its share of federal resources also indicates the role achievement is playing in the regional competition for resources retained by the centre. Thus, control of headship of state is therefore irrelevant. It is relevant where it is possible as it could have been under the military for which there is no documented evidence to use headship of state to divert resources through grants in an arbitrary fashion to their 'home' region.

The other relevance of control of federal power is the quest for individual access to centralized resources and oiling of ethno-clientelism involving 'vertically mobilized groups' (Joseph 1983:30). The 'Kaduna Mafia' exemplifies this. The Northern emirate's class elements seeking to convert their political power into economic power used mobilization around a monolithic north, whipping up fear of southern domination and religious sentiment, inputting government policy in favour of the inner core, incorporation of non-emirate northern elite through selective reward and punishment, etc., towards this end (Takaya 1987). As Ekeh (1996) argued, the military dictatorship in Nigeria benefited the Fulani oligarchy the most. Corrupt power may, in fact, be the greatest instrument of group access to public resources. However, acts of corruption cannot be used to calculate the distribution of federal presence because of the difficulty in proving repatriation to the ethno-region. Nevertheless, they indicate that the greater gainer or loser conclusions of this study remain partial about regional distribution of federal spending or presence. A lot of public resources have been siphoned off to private pockets by acts of corruption and justified as the group's share. Such acts have been perpetrated by individuals of various ethnic backgrounds. It was only a question of more access to political power. Petroleum smuggling and commercial fraud have served as channels for primitive accumulation outside of public expenditure for military officers and civilians (Lewis 1996; Turner 1978; Forrest 1986; Osoba 1996).

Consequently, achievement rather than ascription is the key to access to federal spending formally executed. It rewards no groups which lack a drive for achievement or competitive requisites to support the concentration of resources at the centre. Neither is centralizing resources for providing certain services a useful instrument for taming the ambition of groups so disposed. It rather unwittingly subsidizes the cost of getting such services for them.

The debate on the optimal level of centralization and decentralization remains unsettled. However, there are useful insights from considering the motives of centralization. Centralization is driven by two motives: distribution or redistribution and wider coverage of service delivery. The need for efficiency may be used to rationalize the latter motive. Where the primary motive is redistribution, we can expect those who benefit most from it to turn a blind eye to the issue of equity and the sacrificing of efficiency. There is evidence that distribution is the primary motive of centralization in Nigeria and more especially that fiscal unitarism encouraged by the oil boom was fostered mostly for private accumulation. This is why centralization is widely held to be responsible for poor social service delivery in Nigeria. For example, the 1998 constitutional debate coordinated by Justice Niki Tobi 'held over-concentration of resources in the centre responsible for underdevelopment, political instability, communal violence and a host of other maladies' (Suberu, 2004:35). As Onimode (2000:79) has also argued, fiscal unitarism has 'denied the essential creativity of lower levels and made impossible people-centred and participatory development which must mean self-development, difficult if not impossible'.

Its negative effects are clearly seen in the areas of security, road maintenance, electricity supply, aviation, and education, etc. The failure of centralization is graphically depicted by the contrast between the aesthetic situation of two public spaces – the non-state organization private sector's physical space and the state's physical space. While the former, notably, banks, eating houses, private nursery and secondary schools, is humanizing its space, government has neglected its own, for example, roads, public squares and city centres. Centralization could not have produced better results because its unstated purpose was what Jinadu (2002:33) summarized as the 'packing of northerners at the top' of federal institutions.

This is not to suggest that fiscal decentralization necessarily leads to efficiency (Aleman & Treisman 2002). It does if sub-national governments (state and local) are not corrupt. However inefficiency is certainly worse under centralization as there is no hope of exceptions as under decentralization.

Regional competition based on distribution is antithetical to the evolution of sound public policy and overall national economic development because political alliances are not inspired by progressive national ideology but rather the sheer prospect of securing resources for one's 'own' region. It is antithetical in a more profound sense because it rigidly holds onto sharing principles that are clearly irrational or dysfunctional to economic performance and removes the emphasis on productive competition between regions. At its height, this kind of regional competition leads to political instability, with the threat of disintegration or actual disintegration with usually enormous social dislocation.

Sectional ethnic challenges to the Nigerian State are actually against its centralist bent. They have been mounted for its restructuring. Frustration with the Nigerian State is fundamentally because of its hindrance to individual and group initiatives in generating development by its centralist and reactionary policies. The adoption of the federal institutional framework, in retrospect, fitted the historical differences in governing principles and uneven levels of economic development between regions. With it, each region was unhampered to pursue its development goals during the decade before political independence up until military intervention in Nigerian politics in 1966. Then, the regions did not need the permission of the central government as in civilian unitarism or military dictatorship that eroded federalism later on (Ekeh 1996).

## References

Agiobenebo, T. J., 2003, 'Role of Institutions in Revenue Allocation: OMPADEC and Others', in Akpan H. Ekpo & Enamidem U, Ubok-Udom eds., *Issues in Fiscal Federalism and Revenue Allocation in Nigeria*, Uyo: Department of Economics, University of Uyo, pp. 48-88.

Aleman, E. & Treisman, D., 2002, 'Fiscal Politics in 'Ethnically-Mined', Developing, Federal States: Central Strategies and Secessionist Violence', paper presented at San Diego workshop.

Anusionwu, E. C., 1980, 'The Determinants of Regional Distribution of Primary and Secondary Education in Nigeria', *The Nigerian Journal of Economic and Social Studies*, Vol. 22, No. 1, pp. 3-22.

Bienen, H., 1981, 'The Politics of Income Distribution: Institutions, Class, and Ethnicity' in H. Bienen and V. P. Diejomaoh eds., *The Political Economy of Income Distribution in Nigeria*, New York, London: Holmes and Meier Publishers, Inc.

Ekeh, P. P., 1996, 'The Constitution of Minorities in Nigerian History and Politics', in O. Oyediran, ed., *Governance and Development in Nigeria: essays in honour of Professor Billy J. Dudley*, Ibadan: Agbo Areo Publishers.

Forrest, T, 1986, 'The Political Economy of Civil Rule and the Economic Crisis in Nigeria (1979-84)', *Review of African Political Economy*, Vol. 13, No. 35.

Isumonah, V. A., 2003, 'Planned and Unplanned Outcomes: Uneven and Unsteady Pathways to Democratization in Nigeria', in Julius O. Ihonvbere and John M. Mbaku eds., *Political Liberalization and Democratization in Africa: Lessons from Country Experiences*, Westport, CT: Praeger, pp. 113-139.

Jinadu, L. A., 2002, *Ethnic Conflicts and Federalism in Nigeria*, No.49, ZEF – Discussion Papers on Development, Bonn.

Joseph, R. A., 1983, 'Class, State, and Prebendal Politics in Nigeria', *The Journal of Commonwealth and Comparative Politics*, Vol.21, No.3, pp. 21-37.

Lewis, P., 1996, 'From Prebendalism to Predation: the Political Economy of Decline in Nigeria', *The Journal of Modern African Studies*, Vol. 34, No.1, pp. 79-103.

Odufalu, J., O., 1983, 'The Distribution Impact of Public Enterprises in Nigeria', in H. Bienen and V. P. Diejomaoh eds., *The Political Economy of Income Distribution in Nigeria*, New York, London: Holmes and Meier Publishers, Inc, pp. 455-83.

Onimode, B., 2000, 'Fiscal Federalism in Nigeria: Options for the 21$^{st}$ Century', Research Report.

Osoba, S. O., 1996, 'Corruption in Nigeria: Historical Perspectives', *Review of African Political Economy*, No. 69, pp. 371-386.

Takaya, B. J., 1987, 'Socio-political Forces in the Evolution and Consolidation of the Kaduna Mafia' in B. J. Takaya and S. G. Tyoden, eds., *The Kaduna Mafia*, Jos: Jos University Press Ltd., pp. 29-45.

Suberu, R. T., 2004, 'Pseudo-federalism and the Political Crisis of Revenue Allocation', in Adigun A. B. Agbaje, Larry Diamond and Ebere Onwudiwe, eds., *Nigeria's Struggle for Democracy and good Governance: a festschrift for Oyeleye Oyediran*, Ibadan University Press, Ibadan, pp. 29-46.

Turner, T., 1978, 'Commercial Capitalism and the 1975 Coup', in Keith Pater-Brick ed., *Soldiers and Oil: the political transformation of Nigeria*, London, pp. 166-197.

# Bibliography

Abdulkadir, I. A, 1987, 'Introduction', A. U. Kadiri, ed., *25 Years of Centralizing University Education in Nigeria*, Lagos: NUC, pp. 1-4.

Abernethy, D. B., 1969, *The Political Dilemma of Popular Education: An African Case*, Stanford: The University Press.

Aboyade, O., 1983, *Integrated Economics – a study of developing economies*, London: Addison-Wesley Publishers.

Adamu, M., 1986, 'Withdrawal of Subsidies in the Education System in Nigeria: How Feasible and How Advisable', M. Adamu, ed., *University Education: Its Standard and Relevance to the Nigerian Community – Proceedings of a Joint Seminar Organized by the CVC of Nigerian Universities and the NUC*, Lagos: NUC.

Adebayo, A. G., 1990, 'The Ibadan School and the Handling of Federal Finance in Nigeria', *The Journal of Modern African Studies*, Vol. 28, No. 2, pp. 245-264.

Adedeji, A., 1969, *Nigeria Federal Finance*, London: Hunchinson Educational.

Agiobenebo, T. J., 2003, 'Role of Institutions in Revenue Allocation: OMPADEC and others', Akpan H. Ekpo & Enamidem U, Ubok-Udom, eds., *Issues in Fiscal Federalism and Revenue Allocation in Nigeria*, Uyo: University of Uyo, Department of Economics, pp. 48-88.

Akangbou, Stephen D., 1980, 'The Preliminary Analysis of Recurrent Unit Cost of Higher Education in Nigeria: The Case of the University of Ibadan,' *The Nigerian Journal of Economic and Social Studies*, Vol. 22, No. 3, pp. 395-412.

Ake, Claude, 1994, *Democratization of Disempowerment in Africa*, Lagos: Malthouse

Ake, C. ed., 1986, *Political Economy of Nigeria*, London: Longman.

Akem C., 1994, 'Rethinking Civil Society: Toward Democratic Consolidation', *Journal of Democracy*, Vol. 5, No. 2, pp. 4-17.

All Refer at http://reference.allrefer.com/country-guide-staudy/nigeria74.html

Alli, M.C., 2004, *The Federal Republic of Nigerian Army*, Lagos: Malthouse.

Aleman E. & Treisman, D., 2002, 'Fiscal Politics in "Ethnically-Mined", Developing, Federal States: Central Strategies and Secessionist Violence', paper presented at San Diego workshop.

Alubo, O., 2001, 'The promise and limits of private medicine: health policy dilemmas in Nigeria', *Health Policy and Planning*, Vol. 16, No. 3, pp. 313-321.

Aminu, J, 1987, 'Traffic Warden at Ribadu Road' in A. U. Kadiri, ed., *25 Years of Centralizing University Education in Nigeria*, Lagos: NUC, pp. 8-49.

Angulu, M., 1987, 'Jamb – Were the Critics Right?', in A.U. Kadiri, ed., *25 Years of Centralizing University Education in Nigeria*, Lagos: NUC, pp. 109-113.

Anusionwu, E. Ch., 1980, 'The Determinants of Regional Distribution of Primary and Secondary Education in Nigeria', *The Nigerian Journal of Economic and Social Studies*, Vol. 22, No. 1, pp. 3-22.

Ayodele, O. S., Egwaikhide, F. O., Isumonah, V. A. and Oyeranti, O. A., 2005, 'Supreme Court Judgement and Aftermaths', in Akinola A. Owosekun, Ode Ojowu and Festus O. Egwaikhide, eds., *Contemporary Issues in the Management of the Nigerian Economy*, Ibadan: NISER, pp. 361-382.

Awobajo, S. A., 1981, 'An Analysis of Oil Spill in Nigeria, 1976-1980', paper presented at the seminar on the petroleum industry and Nigerian environment, organized by the Nigeria National Petroleum Corporation (NNPC) at the Petroleum Training Institute (PTI), Warri, 9-12 December.

Bates, R. H., 1974, 'Ethnic Competition and Modernization in Contemporary Africa', *Comparative Political Studies*, Vol. 6, No. 4, pp. 457-484.

Bienen, H., 1981, 'The Politics of Income Distribution: Institutions, Class, and Ethnicity', H. Bienen and V. P. Diejomaoh, eds., *The Political Economy of Income Distribution in Nigeria*, New York, London: Holmes and Meier Publishers, Inc., pp. XXX

Bienen, H., 1983, 'The State and Ethnicity: Integrative Formulas in Africa', in D. Rothchild and V. Olorunsola, eds., *State Versus Ethnic Claims*, Boulder: Westview.

Briggs, B., 1980, 'Federal Character and Higher Education in Nigeria', *Bulletin of the National Universities Commission*, Lagos, July-September, Vol. II, No. 2, pp. 47-74.

Chabal, P. and Daloz, J. P., 1999, *Africa Works: Disorder as Political Instrument*, Oxford: James Currey and Bloomington & Indianapolis: Indiana University Press.

Central Bank of Nigeria, *Annual Report and Statement of Accounts* (various issues).

Chick, A. L., 1953, 'Report of the Fiscal Commissioner on Financial Effects of Proposed New Constitutional Arrangements', Lagos: Government Printer.

Conlan, T., 1998, *From New Federalism to Devolution: Twenty-five years of Intergovernmental Reform*, Washington, D.C.: Brookings Institution Press.

Dahrendorf, R., 1988, *The Modern Social Conflict: An Essay on the Politics of Liberty*, Berkeley, Los Angeles: University of California Press.

Diamond, L., 1987, 'Class Formation in the Swollen African State', *Journal of Modern African Studies*, Vol. 24, No. 4, pp. 567-596.

Due, J. F. and Friedlaender, A. F., 1977, *Government Finance: Economics of the Public Sector*, Illinois: D. Richard.

Egwaikhide, F. O., 1996, 'The Distributional Pattern of Revenues from the Federation Account and the Principle of Derivation in Nigeria', *Administrative Change*, Vol. XXIII, Nos. 1-2, pp. 106-115.

Egwaikhide, F. O. and Aregbeyen, O., 1999, 'Oil Production Externalities in the Niger Delta: Is Fiscal Solution Feasible?', *Proceedings of the 1999 Annual Conference of the Nigerian Economic Society*, pp. 101-115.

Ekeh, P. P., 1975, 'Colonialism and the Two Publics in Africa: A Theoretical Statement', *Comparative Studies in Society and History*, Vol. 17, No. 1, pp. 91-112.

Ekeh, P. P., 2000, 'Nigerian Political History and the Foundations of Nigerian Federalism', *Annals of the Social Science Academy of Nigeria*, No. 12, pp. 1-16.

Ekeh, P. P., 1996, 'The Constitution of Minorities in Nigerian History and Politics', O. Oyediran, ed., *Governance and Development in Nigeria: Essays in Honour of Professor Billy J. Dudley*, (Ibadan, 1996), pp. XXX

Ekpo, A. H. and Ndebbio, J. E. U., 1998, *Local government fiscal operations in Nigeria*, Nairobi: African Economic Research Consortium.

Emenuga, C., 1993, 'Nigeria: The Search for an Acceptable Revenue Allocation Formula', *Proceedings of the 1993 Annual Conference of the Nigerian Economic Society*, pp. 79-105.

Fafunwa, A. B., 1994, *History of Education in Nigeria, New Edition*, Ibadan: NPS Educational Publishers Ltd.

Federal Government of Nigeria, 1977, *Reports of the Presidential Commission on Revenue Allocation, Vol.1: Main Report*, Lagos: Federal Government Press.

Federal Government of Nigeria, 1987, *Political Bureau Report*, Lagos: Federal Government Press.

Filani, M. O., 1981, 'Towards More Efficient Transport Networks in Nigeria', *The Nigerian Journal of Economic and Social Studies*, Vol. 23, No. 2, pp. 209-224.

Forrest, T., 1995, *Politics and Economic Development in Nigeria*, Boulder, Colorado: Westview Press.

Forrest, T., 1986, 'The Political Economy of Civil Rule and the Economic Crisis in Nigeria (1979-84)', *Review of African Political Economy*, Vol. 13, No. 35, pp. 4-26.

Gana, A. T., 2003, 'Federalism and the National Question in Nigeria: A Theoretical Exploration,' in Aaron T. Gana and Samuel G. Egwu, eds., *Federalism in Africa Vol.1: Framing the National Question*, Trenton, NJ and Asmara, Eritrea: Africa World Press, Inc., pp. 143-160.

Grove, A. T., 1951, 'Soil Erosion and Population Problems in South-East Nigeria', *The Geographical Journal*, Vol. 117, No. 3, pp. 291-304.

Gurr, T. R., 1993, *Minorities at Risk: A Global View of Ethnopolitical Conflicts*, Washington, DC: United States Institute of Peace.

Hicks, J. R. and Phillipson, S., 1951, *Report of the Commission on Revenue Allocation*, Lagos: Government Printer.

Hoetink, H., 1975, 'Resource Competition, Monopoly, and Socio-racial Diversity', in Leo A. Despres, ed., *Ethnicity and Resource Competition in Plural Societies*, Muonton Publishers, pp. 9-25.

Hutchful, E., 1970, 'Oil Companies and Environmental Pollution in Nigeria', in Ake, C., ed., *Political Economy of Nigeria*, London: Longman, Chapter 7.

Ike, V. C., 1986, 'A Critique of Admission and Pedagogical Policies and Practices in the Nigerian University', in Mahdi Adamu, ed., *University Education: Its Standard and Relevance to the Nigerian Community – Proceedings of a Joint Seminar Organized by the CVC of Nigerian Universities and the NUC*, Lagos: NUC, pp. 146-160.

Ikporukpo, C. O., 1996, 'Federalism, political power, and the economic power game: conflict over access to petroleum resources in Nigeria', *Environment and Planning C: Government and Policy*, Vol. 14, pp. 159-177.

Ikporukpo, C. O., 1998, 'Transport Studies', Olusegun Areola and Stanley I. Okafor, eds., *50 Years of Geography in Nigeria: The Ibadan Story*, Ibadan: Ibadan University Press, pp. 135-156.

Ikime, O., 2002, 'The Nigerian Civil War and the National Question: A Historical Analysis', in Eghosa E. Osaghae, E. Nwudiwe & R.T. Suberu, eds., *The Civil War and Aftermath*, Ibadan: Program on Ethnic and Federal Studies, pp. 52-73.

Isumonah, V. A., 2003, 'Land Tenure, Migration, Citizenship and Communal Conflicts in Africa', *Nationalism and Ethnic Politics*, Vol. 9, No. 1, Spring, pp. 1-19.

Isumonah, V. A., 2003, 2004, 'The Making of the Ogoni Ethnic Group', *Africa: Journal of the International African Institute*, London, Vol. 74, No. 3, pp. 433-453.

Isumonah, V. A., 2003, 'Planned and Unplanned Outcomes: Uneven and Unsteady Pathways to Democratization in Nigeria', in Julius O. Ihonvbere and John M. Mbaku, eds., *Political Liberalization and Democratization in Africa: Lessons from Country Experiences*, Westport, CT: Praeger, pp. 113-139.

Isumonah, V. A., 2003, (Forthcoming), 'The Fallacy of States' Dependence on the Centre'.

Isumonah, V. A. and Egwaikhide, F. O., 2005, 'The Use of Agencies in Ethno-regional Struggle for Resources in Nigeria', (forthcoming in *African Journal of Political Science*).

Jinadu, L. A., 2002, *Ethnic Conflicts and Federalism in Nigeria*, No. 49, ZEF – discussion papers on development, Bonn.

Joseph, R. A., 1981, 'Democratization under Military Tutelage: Crisis and Consensus in the Nigerian 1979 Elections', *Comparative Politics*, pp. 75-100.

Joseph, R. A., 1983, 'Class, State, and Prebendal Politics in Nigeria', *The Journal of Commonwealth and Comparative Politics*, Vol. 21, No. 3, pp. 21-37.

Kadiri, A. U., ed., *25 Years of Centralizing University Education in Nigeria*, Lagos: NUC, pp. 114-125.

Kasfir, N., 1981, 'Relating Class to State in Africa', *The Journal of Commonwealth and Comparative Politics*, Vol. 21, No. 3, pp. 1-20.

Lewis, P., 1996, 'From Prebendalism to Predation: the Political Economy of Decline in Nigeria', *The Journal of Modern African Studies*, Vol. 34, No. 1, pp. 79-103.

Maiz, R., 2003, 'Politics and Nation: Nationalist Mobilization of Ethnic Differences' *Nations and Nationalism*, Vol. 9, No. 2, pp. 195-212.

Mamdani, M., 2000, 'Beyond Settler and Native as Political Identities: Overcoming the Political Legacy of Colonialism' in Centre for Advanced Social Science CASS, *Ideology and African Development, Proceedings of the Third Memorial Programme in honour of Professor Claude Ake*, Port Harcourt: CASS, pp. 4-22.

Mbanefoh, G. F., 1986, 'Military Presence and the Future of Nigerian Fiscal Federalism', *Faculty of The Social Sciences Lecture Series*, No.1 , University of Ibadan, Ibadan.

Mbanefoh, G. F., 1993, 'Unsettled Issues in Nigerian Fiscal Federalism and the National Question', *Proceedings of the 1993 Annual Conference of the Nigerian Economic Society*, Ibadan: Nigerian Economic Society, pp. 61-77.

Mbanefoh, G. F., 1980, 'Sharing the Costs and Benefits of University Education in Nigeria: A Suggested Approach', *The Nigerian Journal of Economic and Social Studies*, Vol. 22, No.1, pp. 67-83.

Mbanefoh, G. F and Egwaikhide, F. O., 1998, 'Revenue Allocation in Nigeria: Derivation Principle Revisited', in K., Amuwo, A. A. Agbaje, R. T. Suberu and G. Herault, eds., *Federalism and Political Restructuring in Nigeria*, Ibadan: Spetrum Books and Institute Francais de Recherche en Afrique (IFRA), Chap. 14.

Moore, M., 2004, 'Revenues, State Formation and the Quality of Governance in Developing Countries', *International Political Science Review*, Vol. 25, No. 3, pp. 297-319.

Musgrave, R. A., 1969, 'Theories of Federalism', *Public Finance*, Vol. 24, pp. 521-532.

Musgrave R. A. and Musgrave, P. B., 1980, *Public Finance in Theory and Practice*, Tokyo: McGraw-Hill.

National Universities Commission Secretariat, 1987, 'Historical Evolution of the National Universities Commission (the Secretariat and the Board) 1962-1988', A. U. Kadiri, ed., *25 Years of Centralizing University Education in Nigeria*, Lagos: NUC, pp. 114-125.

Nnoli, O., 1980, *Ethnic Politics in Nigeria*, Enugu: Fourth Dimension Press.

Ogbuagu, C. S. A., 1985, 'The Politics of Industrial Location in Nigeria', *Africa Development*, Vol. 10, No.1, pp. 97-122.

Norregaard, J., 1995, 'Intergovernmental Fiscal Relations', in Shome, P., ed., *Tax Policy Handbook*, Washington DC: International Monetary Fund, pp. 247-253.

Odeleye, J. A., (n.d), *Improved Road Traffic Environment for Better Child Safety in Nigeria* - 13th ICTCT workshop.

Odufalu, J. O., 1983, 'The Distribution Impact of Public Enterprises in Nigeria', in H., Bienen and V. P., Diejomaoh, eds., *The Political Economy of Income Distribution in Nigeria*, New York, London: Holmes and Meier Publishers, Inc, pp. 455-83.

Osoba, S. O., 1996, 'Corruption in Nigeria: Historical Perspectives', *Review of African Political Economy*, Vol. 23, No. 69, pp. 371-386.

Ogunbekun, I., Ogunbeku, N. and Orobaton, N., 1999, 'Private Health Care in Nigeria: Walking the Tightrope', *Health Policy and Planning*, Vol. 14, No. 2, pp. 174-181.

Ogunjumo, A., 1983, 'Alternative Frameworks for Understanding the Patterns of Transportation Development in Nigeria', *The Nigerian Geographical Journal*, Vol. 26, Nos. 1&2, pp. 171-197.

Okafor, S.I., 1982, 'Policy and Practice: the Case of Medical Facilities in Nigeria', *Social Science and Medicine*, Vol. 16, No. 22, pp. 71-77.

Okigbo, P. C. N., 1965, *Nigerian Public Finance*, London: Longmans.

Okigbo, P., 1980, *Report of the Revenue Allocation Commission*, Lagos: Government Printer.

Oladapo, I. O., 1986, 'The Emergence of State and Private Universities', A.U. Kadiri, ed., *25 Years of Centralizing University Education in Nigeria*, Lagos: NUC, pp. 59-73.

Onimode, B., 2000, 'Fiscal Federalism in Nigeria: Options for the 21st Century', research report.

Oyovbaire, S. E., 1985, *Federalism in Nigeria: A Study in the Development of the Nigerian State*, London: Macmillan Publishers.

Otite, O., 1990, 'Ethnic Pluralism and Ethnicity in Nigeria (With Comparative Materials)', Ibadan: Shaneson C. I. Ltd.

Phillips, A. O., 1971, 'Nigeria's Federal Financial Experience', *The Journal of Modern African Studies*, Vol. 9, No. 3, pp. 389-408

Phillips, A. O., 1975, 'Revenue Allocation in Nigeria 1970-80', *The Nigerian Journal of Economics and Social Studies*, Vol. 17, No.1, pp. 1-28.

Phillipson, S., 1948, *Administrative and Financial Procedure under the New Constitution: Financial Relations Between the Government of Nigeria and the Native Administration*, Lagos: Government Printer.

Premdas Ralph, R., 1995, *Ethnic Conflict and Development: Case of Guyana*, Aldershot: Avebury.

Raiseman, J. and Tress, R. C., 1958, *Preliminary Report of the Fiscal Commission*, Lagos: Government Printer.

Reno, W., 1993, 'Old Brigades, Money Bags, New Breeds, and the Ironies of Reform in Nigeria', *Canadian Journal of African Studies*, Vol. 27, No.1, pp. 65-87.

Rupley, L., 1981, 'Revenue Sharing in the Nigerian Federation', *The Journal of Modern African Studies*, Vol. 19, No. 2, pp. 258-277.

Schwarz, W., 1968, *Nigeria*, London: Pall Mall Press.

Steel, R. W., Raeburn, C., Dixey, F., Masefield, G. B., Harrison Church, R. J., Jones, G. I., Stamp, L. D. and Grove, A. T., 1951, 'Soil Erosion and Population Problems in South-East Nigeria: Discussion', *The Geographical Journal*, Vol. 117, No. 3, pp. 304-306.

Stewart, F. and Ghani, E., 1991, 'How Significant are Externalities for Development?', *World Development*, Vol. 19, pp. 569-594.

Suberu, R. T., 1994, '1991, State and Local Government Reorganizations in Nigeria', Ibadan: IFRA.

Suberu, R. T., 2004, 'Pseudo-federalism and the Political Crisis of Revenue Allocation', Adigun A. B. Agbaje, Larry Diamond and Ebere Onwudiwe, eds., *Nigeria's Struggle for Democracy and Good Governance: a Festschrift for Oyeleye Oyediran*, Ibadan University Press, Ibadan , pp. 29-46.

Takaya, B. J., 1987, 'Socio-political Forces in the Evolution and Consolidation of the Kaduna Mafia' in B. J. Takaya and S. G. Tyoden, eds., *The Kaduna Mafia*, Jos: Jos University Press Ltd., pp. 29-45.

Tamuno, Tekena N., 1987, 'Management of the Universities in Nigeria: A Look at the Past, the Present and the Future', NUC, *Resource Management in the University System, Proceedings of the NUC-CVC-BC International Seminar*, Lagos: NUC, pp. 15-29.

Tanzi, Vito, 1996, 'Fiscal Federalism and Decentralization: A Review of Some Efficiency and Macroeconomic Aspects' *1996 The International Bank for Reconstruction and Development/ The World Bank Report*, Washington, D.C., pp. 295-316.

Teriba, O., 1966, 'Nigeria Revenue Allocation Experience', *The Nigerian Journal of Economics and Social Studies*, Vol. 8, No.3, pp. 361-382.

Turner, T., 1978, 'Commercial Capitalism and the 1975 Coup', in Keith Pater-Brick, ed., *Soldiers and Oil: the political transformation of Nigeria*, London: Frank Cass and Co., pp. 166-197.

Ukwu, I. U., 1987, 'Federal Financing of Projects for National Development and Integration', in Ukwu, I. Ukwu, ed., *Federal Character and National Integration in Nigeria*, Kuru, Jos: National Institute for Policy and Strategic Studies, pp. 113-129.

Wibbels, E., 2003, 'Bailouts, Budget Constraints and Leviathans: Comparative Federalism and Lessons from the Early United States', *Comparative Political Studies*, Vol. 36, No.5, pp. 475-508.

Williams, G., 1980, *State and Society in Nigeria*, Idanre: Afrografika Publishers.

Yoloye, E. A., 1989, 'Federal Character and Institutions of Higher Learning', P. P. Ekeh & E. E. Osaghae, eds., *Federal Character and Federalism in Nigeria*, Ibadan: Heinemann Educational Books Ltd.

Young, M. C., 1981, The African University: Universalism, Development, and Ethnicity', *Comparative Education Review*, Vol. 25, No. 2. pp. 145-163.

Young, M. C., 1976, *The Politics of Cultural Pluralism*, Madison: University of Wisconsin Press.

www.ingramcontent.com/pod-product-compliance
Lightning Source LLC
Chambersburg PA
CBHW021821270326
41932CB00007B/287